GET YOUR MIND RIGHT

10 LESSONS TO LEAD YOU TOWARDS SUCCESS

BY
H.S. REED, JR.

Bro. Donald,

Thank you for supporting my vision. I truly believe these lessons will work for you as they have for me.

GROOVE EZ

[signature]

"ICE"
2018

GET YOUR MIND RIGHT

10 LESSONS TO LEAD YOU TOWARDS SUCCESS

BY
H.S. REED, JR.

To Taria, A.J. & Justin.

WARNING:

This book is for those who are looking to commit to making

themselves better *NOW.* Even though you are holding yourself

accountable to no one other than yourself,

by doing so ... keep in mind that

the universe is watching and you shall be rewarded accordingly.

If you are of the belief that your future begins *TODAY,* and you are

committed to making every day better than the last by making little

changes within yourself, then take the following pledge and put your

name to it.

PLEDGE OF ALLEGIANCE

(Write your name here)

I,_____ PLEDGE ALLEGIANCE TO MY DREAMS IN

THAT THEY WILL BECOME THE GOALS THAT WILL LEAD ME TO

SUCCESS; FOR NO MATTER WHAT ANYONE HAS TO SAY, I KNOW IN

MY HEART OF HEART AND MY SOUL OF SOULS, THAT WITH FAITH IN

MY CREATOR AND IN MYSELF, I AM DESTINED TO ACHIEVE

WHATEVER I SET MY MIND, HEART AND BODY TO ACHIEVE.

Today's Date:

_____

TABLE OF CONTENTS

INTRODUCTION

INTRODUCTION

In the wee early hours of August in 2005, I had what many might call an epiphany. It was at that moment, sitting in my "man cave" that I knew I had to change the direction of my life. I had no idea how. I had no idea in which direction, but I just **knew in my soul** that a change had to be made.

It was then that I said to myself, ***"I have to get my mind right so I can get my money right."*** Right then and there, I made a conscious decision to begin picking up books. The first book I picked up was "Rich Dad Poor Dad" by Robert Kiyosaki, and ***get my mind right*** is exactly what that book did. The lessons I learned in that book set me on a path that brought about the changes that had to be made in my life. Some of those changes were wonderful and others quite painful. But in the end, I came out on top, living a life that many are kinda' jealous of!

I share more detail about those changes in my first two books, "FIND A WAY TO MAKE A WAY!" and "SUCCESS IS A JOURNEY." What I will say here is this, I began reading a series of books all with the goal of ***"getting my mind right."*** As I was "finding my way," I was inspired to share the life lessons I had learned up to that point, and as I applied the new lessons I was learning, I began to experience some "success on my journey," and I was inspired to share even more of the life lessons I was learning. And even though I'm still learning and still growing, I feel like I've finally gotten my mind right and I'm inspired to share even more of the life lessons I have learned.

So here you have ***"GET YOUR MIND RIGHT"*** in your hands. If you've never met me, if you don't follow me on social media, or if you haven't read my first two books, you might not be prepared for my writing style. In a word, I'm very **blunt**. In two words, this book is a ***no nonsense*** approach to personal development.

I often tell people that I am not your typical happy shiny kind of motivational speaker. I am not in the business of begging people to improve themselves. I am not in the business of pulling up people who prefer to stay where they are and do nothing to pull themselves up. The astrophysicist, Dr. Neil deGrasse Tyson said, "It's okay to remind people to pull themselves up by the bootstraps... Just remember that some people have no boots." I say it's okay if you don't have any boots, but if you go through life barefoot you have no one but yourself to blame.

This world, this life, is full of opportunities. One of life's biggest misconceptions is that if you wait long enough, at some point opportunity will come knocking. The reality is that the people who are waiting for opportunity are doing just that... waiting. However, those select few who made the decision to **get their minds right** know that you don't wait for opportunity... You track opportunity down like Dog the Bounty Hunter! You don't wait for opportunity to come knocking... **You find out where it is and you kick its door down and take what's meant to be yours!**

So let us begin. If you skipped the warning a couple pages back, go back and read it. So you know what you're getting yourself into. If you haven't read and signed the contract (with yourself) on the page after the warning, go back, read and sign it so that you know you are making a pact – not with me, but with yourself. If you give up, you're not really giving up on me... you're giving up on yourself. But we both know you're a bigger and better person than that. It is my most sincere hope that as you read these pages and finish this book you are one huge step closer on your mission to **GET YOUR MIND RIGHT.**

"AUDACES FORTUNA IUVAT"
(Fortune Favors the Brave!)

Chapter One
10 Questions to Help You Start to Get Your Mind Right

Question #1:
WHY DO YOU DO THE WORK THAT YOU DO?

There are 3 vocational categories: a **Job**, a **Career**, and a **Calling**.

JOB

Having a job is basically an arrangement between you and your employer in which you trade your hours and labor for dollars, and more often than not, your employer determines the value of your hours and labor by how much he or she pays you. If you work well enough you may receive promotions, raises and bonuses. On the other hand, if your work is poor, your employer may dock your pay, reduce it, or terminate your employment altogether.

In my life I have lived in all three categories. When I was scrambling to find my way, I had a whole bunch of jobs. I even remember times when I would get a job working for a security company and I would still be looking through the Classifieds for another job (this was obviously about a good 20 years before LinkedIn, Craig's List and jobs requiring people to apply online).

There is no loyalty in having a job. Well, you're loyal to the extent that you will work to get paid, but if a better job comes along you know you'll be on the first thing smoking to get to it. "Job security" is a myth because if your employer has to cut expenses, you could find yourself and your paycheck as one of those expenses... CUT.

CAREER

A career is a vocation you sought and acquired education and training to perform. It is the one thing you do because it gives you a sense of purpose. You can turn a job into a career, but only when you begin to treat your job as more than a job. When you begin to exhibit loyalty to your job and commit yourself to being more than just a clock-puncher, you can begin turning your job into a career.

When you begin showing initiative by coming in early and staying late, voluntarily taking on more duties, and putting in for more training in what you're currently doing or advanced training in what you'd like to be doing, you know you're pursuing a career.

For about five years before I became a cop I was trying to become a cop. Like I said earlier, I had a whole bunch of jobs during that time. I was able to go from "flashlight rent-a-cop" security jobs to working in retail Loss Prevention. My last "job" before becoming a cop was working for the Old Navy clothing store. At the time, it seemed like my dream of becoming a cop just wasn't going to come true, so I began to turn my job into a career.

I dedicated myself to Old Navy. I put myself up for the assignments no one else wanted. I even began buying more clothes from the store. After a while, I began catching the eye of management. I was even flown to Maryland by Old Navy to train newly hired Loss Prevention Agents at a Baltimore location. When a (then) new store was being built and opening up in North Bergen, NJ, I applied for the Lead Agent position.

This raised a couple of eyebrows because I was working at the New Jersey "flagship" store in Paramus. When asked why I would give up such a great location, I told my interviewer that if I were going to grow within the company I needed to be someplace where I could plant my own flag and prove myself.

You see, I wasn't the senior agent in Paramus and the guy who was, was actively trying to sabotage me whenever he could. But I was focused on making something happen for myself with Old Navy. I was preparing to go back to school, and Gap Inc. (Old Navy's parent company) was going to pay for it. As things turned out, I got that Lead Agent position.

I was making moves towards management. I had my own team of agents under me, and we were making great progress. Then something funny happened... I got hired by the East Orange Police Department. Two years after that I was hired by the Woodbridge Police Department where I completed my career.

I went from having jobs, to having a job that was turning into a career, to having a career. However, Law Enforcement was what I really wanted to do, and the funny thing is, I had actually accepted that it just wasn't going to happen. When it did, I jumped on it. I don't know what or where I would be had I decided to stay at Old Navy, but I can assure you that you wouldn't be reading this book because there would have been no call for it to have been written. What made this possible was because all of the twists and turns on my journey led me to my...

CALLING

A calling is almost identical to a career in that there will likely be education and training involved and it gives you a sense of purpose, but there's one exception... You would do what you do for the sake of doing it with little regard for financial compensation. The funny thing about answering and following your calling is that you may reach a point where people see so much value in what you do that they will pay you; and pay you well, to do it.

I worked so hard and so long to become a police officer that I believed that it was my calling. I was trained extensively, it gave me a sense of purpose, and starting out my salary was not all that great. But I LOVED what I was doing.

For me it wasn't about the foot chases (I hated running) and lock-ups. What I loved most about the job was that I was helping people. I can say I've pulled people out of burning houses. I've comforted families when a loved one died – whether it was expected or sudden and unexpected. I have mentored young people and changed their paths from the streets to college. But as much as I loved my job – oops ... my career (smile), I discovered that it was not my calling.

I hadn't recognized or heard it yet, but my calling came to me one late night after "saving the world" via my Sony PlayStation and a voice in my head asked me, ***"Well congratulations... Now what do you have to show for it?"*** I had no answer, and that in and of itself was the answer – nothing. I had nothing to show for it. So I made a decision that night – or rather ***early*** that morning – to put my PlayStation down and pick up some books. My goal was to ***get my mind*** right so I could get my money right.

The first book I picked up was "Rich Dad Poor Dad" by Robert T. Kiyosaki, and that book began opening my ears so I could be on the right frequency to hear my calling; well, calling out to me. From that book alone I was inspired to start my own business (even though I had no idea what it would be at that time), change my thinking about money (which resulted in me buying a house a year later), and give me the initial practical knowledge and insight to motivate my wife to start her own business (which actually became the catalyst of me deciding that my business would be Motivational Speaking).

There's a saying that goes, "If you want to hear God laugh, tell Him what you've got planned." And there's a line in Tyler Perry's movie "Diary of a Mad Black Woman," in which one of the characters says, "God has the power to show you just who is God." Well, that's just what happened to me. I told God my plans. He had a good laugh. He showed me just who God was, and He made it possible for me to answer my calling.

You see, when I knew I wanted to become a professional motivational speaker, **my plan** was to develop myself as a speaker during my Law Enforcement career – which had a shelf life of about 20 more years at the time, and then upon retiring, seamlessly transcend over into speaking as my "new" career. That was **my plan**, and man oh man was God listening!

I began reading, studying and training to become a speaker. I put myself out there and began getting a few engagements. I made $150 cash from my very first speech and I only spoke for 20 minutes! What was crazy about that wasn't so much the amount of money for so little time, but I specifically told the client that I would speak for free! When I got home and opened the "thank you" card that I had been given and found the cash inside, my mind began crunching numbers. I thought, "If I could make $150 for 20 minutes that means I could very well charge at least $450 to speak for an hour! At that point *I KNEW* that speaking was what I wanted to do with my life.

Then God started to do His thing, but I didn't recognize it as such during the time. In 2007, I was involved in a head-on car accident while on duty. I walked away sore and bruised, but three months later; on the day before New Year's Eve, I was called into my Captain's office and told that one of the women who was in the car that collided with my squad car died in the hospital. I was shattered. I was allowed to go home and take a few days off. But I stuffed the pain I was feeling away and I went back to work after two days. A couple days into the New Year, I was informed that I would be taken off the road while the collision was further investigated.

For a little over six months I was working inside on the radio dispatching calls to the officers on the road. At the conclusion of the investigation, I was blamed for having caused the collision even though I had my overhead lights on and I was swerving to avoid a car that had come out in front of me. I was looking at a 90 day suspension without pay which would have cost me about $50,000 of my salary. A hit my family could not afford to take.

However, my attorney was able to work out a deal which, in lieu of being suspended without pay, I forfeited all of my remaining vacation days and for the rest of the year I would work an extra day. At the end of the year, the "overtime" that was accumulated from those extra days worked was all taken back by the department. By the time I got back on the road, I wasn't the same. I had no enthusiasm. The "career" that *I thought* was a "calling" had become a "job." I was trading hours for dollars.

Remember that pain I told you I stuffed away? Well, like any real pain, you can't really stuff it away. You can't run from it. You can deny it exists, but that doesn't mean it doesn't exist. It just began manifesting itself in a bunch of different ways. I was using my motivational speaking to hide it. I even wrote the first manuscript for my second book, "Success is a Journey" during that period. But the pain was still there. It affected how I performed on the job and it affected how I behaved as a husband. Let's just say I was "going through the motions" of doing both, but I found no joy in either.

I reached a point where I really needed to do something or else I would lose everything. I went to my union representative and told him I needed to talk to someone. Now let me pause for a moment. Cops are expected not to feel pain. Cops are expected to go from one job to the next and just do it. Fatal accident? Do the job and move on. Dealt with a rape victim? Do the job and move on. Someone died in their home or jumped in front of a train? Do the job and move on. People tend to forget or ignore the fact that *cops are people too.*

Many cops deal with these things in different ways, some productive and others not so much. One thing is for certain... When a cop actually reaches out and asks for help, you get him or her some help! A lot of cops have "eaten their guns" (taken their own lives) because they felt they had no one they could talk to and or no other options in life but to end the pain by ending their lives.

My union rep was "old school police" and he knew some guys that had taken that route throughout his career. He arranged for me to speak to a therapist, and believe it or not, on my way to her office for my first meeting – five minutes away from her office – I got into a car accident! Someone smacked right into the side rear of my car as I was making a turn. My wife came and picked me up from the scene and took me to the therapist's office. I was a total wreck emotionally. After a couple more meetings, she diagnosed me with having PTSD (Post-Traumatic Stress Disorder) all stemming from that first accident back in 2007. She also recommended that I apply for early retirement under those grounds.

My department accepted my request and I was scheduled to end my career on May 1st of 2011. From that first meeting in October of 2010 throughout the months leading to my retirement, I was "in therapy." Friend, let me tell you, it was *not* fun. My therapist had me climbing the walls sometimes, but she had to pull out all of the negativity that I had been suppressing – not just since that accident – but throughout my life!

By the time my retirement date rolled around, there was no determination made about my pension – the money I would have to live on and continue to support my family with. It turned out that someone" in my department went to someone they knew on the pension board and told them I was faking having PTSD and that because I was a motivational speaker on the side, I couldn't possibly have PTSD.

As a result of this act of treachery, I wound up going from May (my retirement) to November of 2011 with *no pay whatsoever.* I had some money saved up and got some help from family, but damned if I wasn't going through it inside during that time. Even though the bills were being paid, I did not feel I was the man I was supposed to be, and even while still "in therapy" I was severely depressed, and yes I did on occasion have suicidal thoughts.

I credit three things for keeping me going day after day, week after week, and month after month:

1. I have always believed that suicide is a "permanent solution to a temporary problem."
2. I have two boys who I have to make men out of, and it would be sheer cowardice to take myself out and leave my wife with the burden of having to take on that job alone.
3. **Faith** that God would see me through.

I began to use a couple of affirmations I had picked up in my motivational studies… "If you're going through hell, **keep on going!**" and "If you've reached the end of your rope, tie a knot into it and hang on!" By the time it was all said and done, I was granted my full pension **and back-pay** from May 1st through to November. **Now why did I share all of that with you?**

I shared that with you for a few reasons. One, like I said, I told God **my plan**, which was to be a cop for 25 years and **then** be a full-time speaker and author. God showed me just **who was God**, and **my plan** was pretty much scrubbed. Second, to let you know that when you are committed to following your calling, **expect all hell to break loose.**

Like in the biblical story of Job, God will seem to remove His hedge of protection from around you and let the devil have his way with you, to test your faith and your determination. And third, if you keep the faith and stay true to knowing there **is** a light at the end of the tunnel, one day you will reach it and be able to live your purpose.

The way I see it, God saw what I wanted and knew it to be true in my heart, but He just wasn't going to **give** it to me. I had to earn it. I had to prove myself worthy of it. They say in life, it's not so much the hand you're dealt, but how you play that hand that determines the value of your life.

Well, I saw it as my life being a deck of cards and all that drama I went through as God shuffling the deck and dealing me new hands. Like any good game of cards, some hands play out well and others not so much, but I learn from the bad hands and *I keep on playing!* Whether you have a job, career or calling, play like your life depends on it... *because it does!*

Question #2:
WHAT KIND OF WORK WOULD YOU DO IF PAYING BILLS WERE NOT A FACTOR?

Regardless if you have a job, a career, or are following your calling, bills will always be a factor. No matter what, the lights and heat must stay on. The family must be fed. Your home and car have to be paid for and insured. So looking deeper into this question, are you working to fulfil a purpose *other than* paying bills? For many, the honest answer is no. Are you one of that "many?" C'mon... tell the truth!

Because we all have the aforementioned responsibilities and more, it makes no sense to ask "What if you didn't have to pay bills?" It doesn't matter if you are a millionaire or just getting by, there will always be bills that require payment. The seed I want you to plant in the fertile soil of you mind is, **what if your work fulfilled you AND paid your bills?**

You see, when this happens, your bills are not a factor. To use a familiar phrase, it's nothing more than paying "the cost of living." However, what's happening with most people is that they're paying the cost of *surviving*, but in reality can't really afford to *live.*

The truth is if the utility companies and the banks to which you pay your car note, rent or mortgage, etc. are enjoying your money more than you are, then you're just surviving. If this is your situation, is there some way you can do something that provides you more money at the end of the month rather than having **more month at the end of the money?**

Is there a way you can branch off and do for yourself what it is you do for your employer? Is there a talent or skill you have that with a little – or perhaps a lot more commitment, could increase your income?

Let me ask that last question a different way... What skills or talents do you possess, and can you put them to market for yourself? Could you work for Rotor-Rooter as a plumber making $15-$20 an hour or could you have your own plumbing business in which *you* are charging $40-$50 an hour? Could you be a salesperson making 10% commissions on your wares or could you create or buy into a company in which you're the one getting 90% of the sales and doling out the 10% commissions. Real estate agents make anywhere from 2.5% to 3% in commissions. The brokers they're working for might be making twice that *just because they're the broker!* Could *you* become a broker? *What's stopping you?*

Remember, we're talking about the kind of work you could or would be doing if paying bills were not a factor. One of the things I did while I was going through the ordeal of fighting for my pension was take a real estate class and get my real estate license. For one, it kept me busy.

For the five hours I was in class and the three to four hours I spent afterwards at the library studying everything I learned in class that day, I wasn't thinking so much about my ordeal. Like the saying goes, "An idle mind is the devil's workshop." I gave the devil as little time as I possibly could to rot my mind with nonsense.

I was facing a situation in which bills were a major factor, but a "job" or "career" in real estate could have likely become one in which bills were not a factor as I was entering the field during the time that the market was slowly beginning to pick back up. I made a little over twelve hundred dollars off of my first sale because I was "shadowing" a senior agent who was mentoring me. I made a little more from my second sale.

There were agents making $3000 or more in commissions from one sale, and they were selling two or three properties a month. The rear parking lot of the office was lined up with Mercedes Benzes, BMWs and Audis and my shiny 2011 Camaro looked just as nice amongst them.

However, when my pension situation was resolved in my favor, I saw it as being in a position in which I could work on building my speaking, writing and Life Coaching businesses **without bills being a factor.** I then saw my experience for what it really was, something to keep me busy and occupied so that I would not do something stupid.

In addition to the commission I made from my first sale, my broker also reimbursed me for the money I paid for my classes, so I was able to profitably walk away from real estate not having lost any money, having made a few bucks and gained some valuable knowledge along the way. I'd call that a win-win situation!

I would not wish what I was going through at the time on you, but what I was going through was a fire being lit under my bottom to take action to support my family. If you're not happy with your job, or you feel as though there may be something lacking in your career, perhaps that's the fire being lit under your bottom and it's just not hot enough for you to feel the heat. This reminds me of a story I often tell...

A man decides to talk a walk down a country road. About a mile into his walk he gets thirsty and stops by a house where an old man is sitting on the porch. The walker asked the old man for a glass of water and he walks inside to get it. All the while, the old man's hound dog is laying down and howling on the far end of the porch.

The old man comes back and says, "Don't you worry about him." When the walker asks what's wrong with the dog, the old man says, "Oh, he's just sattin' on a nail." When the walker asks why doesn't the dog just get up and move off the nail, the old man says, "Well... I guess it just don't hurt enough."

So let me ask you... Does what you do for a living light a fire in your belly or is it that nail that you're sitting on? Does what you do for a living consume you positively or negatively? If it consumes you positively **and** your bills are getting paid **and** you have money to enjoy afterwards, then you are on a good path.

However, if your "job" consumes you to the point where you are missing out on spending time with your boyfriend/girlfriend, spouse, and or children – **and** you barely have enough money to go to the movies or Buffalo Wild Wings or Joe's Crab Shack, then your "job" is to you what that nail was to the hound dog in the story. You will only take action and make a move to your benefit when it hurts too much.

What I want you to know is that you shouldn't have to wait to that point. Better stated, you should **not** wait until that point. There is always going to be some discomfort involved with bettering yourself, but if you're just going through the stress and discomfort of your job just for a paycheck then you are shortchanging yourself and the ones you love.

Now, in all honesty, let me be clear about something... Just because there is something out there you love to do, that doesn't mean there won't be discomfort involved, but **that** discomfort is what's called good pain. That's the kind of pain spoken of when people say "no pain no gain!" It's like going to the gym, taking a long brisk walk, or running several miles.

When you find yourself doing what you love, you know that pain is only making you stronger. When you're paying those bills, you're just paying the cost of living – **not the cost of surviving**, and when you're doing that, your bills won't matter.

Question #3:
HOW MUCH MONEY DO YOU SPEND
TO IMPROVE YOURSELF?

This question has nothing to do with the amount of money you may spend on cars, clothes, jewelry, your home or any recreational activities. These are things which can be lost practically instantly. Just look at what the victims of Hurricane Katrina, Irene and Sandy lost. Between my wife and me, we lost three cars as a result of Hurricane Sandy, and they were just sitting in the driveway (that shiny 2011 Camaro I was just talking about being one of them). Countless others lost their homes, their businesses, and nearly all if not all of their cherished belongings. In short, they were left with almost nothing **but themselves.**

What would you have within yourself if you lost everything around you? It was Jim Rohn who said, "Pity the man who can tell you his favorite restaurant, but can't tell you his favorite author; for he has a place to feed his body, but no place to feed his mind." What good is it to be able to **look** good but not **feel** good, or actually **be** good? So what we're talking about here is investing your money in yourself. What is truly a sad thing to see in my Coaching practice is when I have a conversation with a potential client, and they see the value in what I have to offer, but they fall back because they believe my services are "too expensive."

Well... Let me honestly say that my services are not cheap. I provide a valuable service, so why would I charge cheap? Certainly, you've heard the saying *"you get what you pay for."* Personally, I strive to give my clients more than what they're paying for because I care that much, but best believe they do pay for what they get before they begin seeing they're actually getting more than what they're paying for. I actually had one of my clients tell me that I wasn't charging her enough!

Yet I digress. My point here is that if you want to improve the quality of your life, it's going to cost you. Most people have a problem when it comes to evaluating what they're getting in relation to what they're paying for. My suggestion is that you seek out what the return is going to be for your "investment."

But here's the thing, you don't have to spend a great amount of money to make lasting improvements in your life. In 1998, I spent about $10-$15 on two books that really changed my life. Those books were "Think & Grow Rich" by Napoleon Hill, and "How to Win Friends & Influence People" by Dale Carnegie. The lessons I learned in those books helped me *get my mind right* at a time in my life when I really needed it.

You may not believe it, but a $20 investment in a "how to" book could put you on the path to making a fortune! In 2005, I spent $20 for Robert Kiyosaki's book, "Rich Dad Poor Dad," and that investment continues to pay off! That $20 led to me inspiring my wife, Taria, to start her own business, which led me to starting my own.

Now we both own our time. We don't have to ask anyone to take a day off. We don't have to wait our turn in seniority to put in for a vacation. Instead of being someplace where someone else tells us how much they're going to pay us per hour, **we tell people what they are going to pay us.**

That was just one book; however, over the years I have invested thousands of dollars in books, audio programs and seminars. Over the years – even before deciding to become a motivational speaker, I read and listened to the likes of Les Brown, Anthony Robbins, Zig Ziglar, Brian Tracy and Jim Rohn to name a few.

These are the teachers who not just inspired me to do better with my life, but also inspired me to inspire others to make their lives better. Taria invested hundreds of dollars in classes, webinars, and seminars to hone her skills in photography. In less than ten years since deciding to start our own businesses we're calling our own shots. The only schedules we have to check ourselves against are one another's.

What areas could or do you want to see yourself doing better? How do you think you're going to do it? Do you think it's going to be free? **Think again!** I'm reminded of the line from the movie (and subsequent TV series), "Fame," in which the dance teacher and choreographer played by Debbie Allen says to her class on the first day, "You got big dreams. You want fame. Well, fame costs... And right here is where you start paying – in sweat."

Improvement costs. If you want to improve your house it's going to cost. If you want to improve your wardrobe it's going to cost. If you want to improve your car it's going to cost. So what makes people think that they can improve themselves – what makes you think you can improve yourself – for free? What is sad is that people will be willing pay those prices to fix or improve their things, but not see the value in paying whatever price is necessary or required to improve themselves.

In closing, I want to ask you again, **how much money do you spend to improve yourself?** I'm not asking to get an exact dollar amount from you, but to get you to ask yourself – and answer yourself! Also, I want you to get into the habit of spending money on improving yourself; on improving **you,** not the things around you. Actor & recording artist,

Will Smith once said, "We spend money that we do not have, on things we do not need, to impress people who do not care." This is very much true in the lives of far too many people. As you continue to read about "getting your mind right," I want you to think about spending the money you do have on the things you do need to impress and improve the only person that really matters in the end… **YOU.**

Question #4:

HOW MUCH MONEY WOULD YOU SPEND TO IMPROVE YOURSELF IF PAYING BILLS WERE NOT A FACTOR?

I have to be honest with you... This is a trick question. It's a trick question because, as stated earlier, bills will always be a factor. Since we will always have bills to pay, the real question is, *is improving yourself just as important – if not more important than paying a bill?*

By no means am I suggesting you should neglect your fiduciary responsibilities and blow your money on books and seminars, but certainly you can forego one movie night and spend that money on two or three books that could teach you something you could do in order to better afford more movie nights or even a tropical vacation.

As I said in the last chapter, I have encountered people who have told me that they could not afford my Coaching fees, but some of these same people go to every concert that comes to town, or they're at the stadium or arena almost every time their favorite sports team has a home game. The thing to look for here is value. They see more value in being at a concert or a game for a couple hours and spending money on gas, tolls, parking, food, drink, and the show or game itself than investing that money in themselves.

Don't get me wrong, I enjoy a good concert myself (on a rare occasion). I'm not a fan of going to sporting events. When I have to go to the bathroom or get something to eat or drink, I'd rather be able to pause the game or wait until the commercial and handle that business without ever having to worry about waiting in lines – or more importantly – the weather. But that's just me. Think about it... think about the total dollar amount you spent at the last game or concert you attended and ask yourself if that money could have been invested elsewhere?

Hell, for what I could spend on one night at the movies – especially the new dine-in theaters where they actually bring food and drinks to my seat which is roughly about $40, I can pay my gym membership for two months!

Again, just as I am not saying you should neglect your bills, I am also not saying you should deprive yourself of recreation. However, the athletes and entertainers you are spending hundreds of dollars to see not only have their money, but they have yours too! Look at it like this... Many actors – Academy award winning actors still have **and pay** coaches who guide them in ways to better improve their skills.

This is them investing in themselves. When you spend your money at the box office, they're making their money back. When they get that 6, 7, or even 8 figure check, they're getting a return on their investment.

Remember what we discussed earlier... Bills will always have to be paid, but when you're making that much money to where you've got plenty left over after all of them are paid, that is what is meant by them not being factor. To paraphrase the James Brown song, you have *"pay the cost to be the boss."* Ultimately, you have to ask yourself – or at least I would like for you to ask yourself, how much are you willing to invest in yourself so that you may someday reach the point where people are spending their money *on you?*

Question #5:
WHAT KIND OF LIFESTYLE WOULD YOU LIVE IF YOU COULD?

This question is applicable to those who are unwilling to settle for where they are and what they have now. It's not a matter of being ungrateful for where you are and what you have, but one big misconception that people have is that "more" is a bad 4-letter word. What's wrong with wanting to own a home if you live in an apartment? What's wrong with wanting a car if you're currently taking the bus? What's wrong with wanting your children to go to private school; or having the ability to take a vacation – not just whenever you like but *wherever* you like?

You don't necessarily have to have a "caviar wishes and champagne dreams" lifestyle, but surely you want more than a "Hamburger Helper" reality, right? So, play along... What kind of lifestyle would you have if you could? You see, one reason why people fail to make their dreams come true is that they fail to believe that their dreams can come true.

Something I always tell my audiences is that **the impossible is only impossible because you have yet to step up and make it possible.** More often than not, the only person who is standing in the way of you living the lifestyle you want or wish you could have is **you.**

This is what getting your mind right is all about. You're going to have to come to some hard realizations about yourself. If you want to make your wishes and your dreams become reality, you're going to have to be the first to believe that they can. You don't have to be the only one who holds that belief, but you have to be **the first one** to hold that belief.

There's something funny about how God, the universe, or whatever you deem your higher power to be works... If you're not the first one to hold that belief rarely will anyone else. And in those cases where someone may see potential in you that you don't see in yourself, if you continue to fail to see it, at some point in time that person may come to the realization, "Hey, maybe I was wrong" and they'll just move on. However, when you hold that belief; as you move forward in working that belief, God will put into your life the ideas, people and resources necessary to keep you moving forward to the achievement of your goals.

The thing to keep in mind here is that there are no limits. There are no boundaries except those you place before yourself. This is what people do. I know this because I have done it myself. We all do it to ourselves. Don't believe me? Have you ever been faced with a choice to do something or had an idea about something you wanted to do or said the words *"that's easier said than done"* to yourself – or worse, have someone you shared your idea with say those words to you?

Then you took those words and used them as a means to give yourself permission to do nothing. The words *"easier said than done"* have probably cheated more people out of their greatness than cancer has ever killed.

So I ask you again... What kind of lifestyle would you live if you could? Take a pen and piece of paper and describe to yourself the life you want to live. What kind of house would you like to live in? What kind of car would you drive? What kind of clothes would you wear? Where would your children go to school? Where would you party on the weekends? Where would you vacation? How many vacations would you take in any given year?

Now, would you like to know how you go about making these things more tangible in your life? Of course you would! The short answer is **you have to work at it.** However, what kind of work you must do depends on what you want to happen. So how about I give you something that I know **you** can do, whomever **you** are. Take that list you just wrote and begin educating yourself about those things. Create a vision board for yourself. Either put one up in your home or create a virtual one on www.Pinterest.com.

That house you described, go online and research how much that kind of home costs. Find out where that kind of house is. There might be one like it in Atlanta, California, Vermont, or Arizona. It doesn't matter. It's **wherever you want it to be.** Research the school systems in those communities. Do they have provide the quality of education you want for your children? That car you want to drive… What do you know about it? Educate yourself about it. How fast can it go? How good on gas is it? What kind of bells and whistles come standard? What kind of options are there? What color interiors are there for you to choose from? How much is the maintenance going to cost you?

Write these things down! Write these things down because the more you know, the better equipped you are to walk into that Realtor's office or that car dealership and tell them what you want instead of them "selling" you whatever is available.

Look up the social life in the communities where that house is – or within a reasonable radius you're willing to travel for an enjoyable evening out. Do celebrities frequent those spots? Look up the hotels in those vacation spots you wrote down? Do you have to fly to get there? Can you drive there? Those clothes you want to wear… What do you know about the designers? Could you wear those clothes and make **them** look better? Write all of these things down!

Don't deny yourself! Go all out! Don't let where you are and what you have today stop you from first dreaming and then believing you can have **more** tomorrow. One of the main reasons people fail to reach or exceed their potential is not because they are shut out or excluded from life's opportunities, but because they exclude themselves.

Just because a door is closed does not mean it's locked and even if it is locked, that does not mean it has to remain locked. You just have to be willing to find the right key. As the scripture says, "Without vision the people will perish." Instead of asking "why me?" when bad things happen, see them as learning experiences designed especially for you to learn from and ask yourself, "why not me?"

You can have the lifestyle you fall into or you can have the lifestyle you create for yourself. There are plenty of people out there waiting and willing to tell you what you can't have and what you're not capable of. There is absolutely no reason why you should be one of them. You don't need a fortune teller. You don't need ESP. You can create your own future. You just have to be willing to work for it. When you create a more detailed picture of what you want for yourself, you will find yourself discovering ways to make those things work for you!

Question #6:
NOW THAT YOU'VE IDENTIFIED THAT LIFESTYLE, WHY CAN'T YOU LIVE IT?

If you did not make your "Lifestyle List," put this book down and do so now. If you could not honestly answer those questions, you can't possibly answer the above question.

The "easy cop out" answer will be "money." I call it an "easy cop out" answer because many will see it as an insurmountable wall. However, here's another question, *how important to you is it to live the lifestyle you outlined?* If the answer is "not important," then you are free to go back to living your current day to day life. But if your answer is that it's very important to live that lifestyle, you have an obligation to yourself and those you love (your spouse and children) to *find a way* to achieve that lifestyle.

Now keep in mind, this is not about becoming rich – unless that is a requirement of the lifestyle you want. Wherever you are in your life, you can have more if you believe you can; however, belief is not enough. As the scripture states, "Faith without works is dead." Your vision is that lifestyle. Your faith is what tells you it can be yours, and your work is what tells you that it will eventually be yours.

Again, more often than not, it's not the person talking to you that will talk you out of your vision. It is the person talking **within you** who will do it. The best way to find out what you are capable or incapable of is to do something – anything that will move you towards that goal or lifestyle. The journey will not be easy, but that is to be expected.

People fail because either they encounter obstacles and quit, or they don't even bother to take action at all. If you answered that your desired lifestyle is important to you, go back to your list and write down **why** each item on that list is important to you. Knowing **why** you want to achieve something is what will guide you to **how** you will achieve it.

Question #7:
WHAT MAKES ANYONE CURRENTLY LIVING THAT LIFESTYLE A BETTER PERSON THAN YOU?

What's separating you from someone who is living how you would like to live? Again, "money" is the easy answer, but I think that we all would agree that the money these people have doesn't make them better than who we are – and contrary to popular belief, you don't have to compromise who you are in order to have more in life. There are plenty of people who will and who do compromise themselves in order to get more.

That's them... that does not have to be *you.* We all have our own paths to follow in life. Look at it like this, we all come out of the womb one at a time, and caskets come one per customer. You can look at what others are doing, but you may or may not have to do what they did to get there yourself. There is more than one way to reach any given destination.

Something that success coach, Jack Canfield, says will always ring true... *"Success leaves clues."* If you have identified the kind of lifestyle you want to live, and why it's important to you to achieve it, then the next step to find out is how you can achieve it in such a way that you can hold your head high and be proud of your achievements. It's not enough to see how someone else is living and want that for yourself. Barring all immoral, illegal and unethical practices, what are you willing to do to achieve that lifestyle?

Is what you're currently doing going to get you where you want to be? Will you require new or additional skills to get to where you want to be? Are you willing to learn something new to achieve your desired lifestyle? What separates the successful from the mediocre or unsuccessful is that those who are successful are open to the mindsets and paradigms that will give them the shift in course they need in order to get on the right track.

For example, being a rapper made Will Smith rich, but shifting gears and changing lanes into acting is what made him wealthy in that he can demand $20 million dollars per movie. In short, it's not *who* these people are, but what they *do* that makes the difference between their lifestyles and yours. The real question then is, what are *you* willing to *do* to achieve that lifestyle?

Question #8:
WHAT WOULD YOU BE WILLING TO GIVE UP OR GIVE AWAY IN ORDER TO BE BETTER TOMORROW THAN YOU ARE TODAY?

It was Albert Einstein who said, "The definition of insanity is doing the same thing again and again while expecting a different outcome each time." Every day people get up and go to a job where they are doing the same thing day after day, week after week, month after month, and year after year – yet many actually wonder why their circumstances never seem to change for the better.

There's another saying that goes, "If you want to keep getting what you're getting, just keep on doing what you're doing." In short, if you want to have more or be more, than what you have or are, then you are going to have to **do** more. It is highly possible that you will also have to do something **different.** You might have to learn a new skillset. You might have to totally abandon the path you're currently on.

You might have to burn some bridges and terminate some relationships. You are in the groove; or perhaps rut, that you are in today because at some point you reached a level of comfort in which you came to know exactly what was required of you and you decided that you were going to meet that requirement. When you found that "sweet spot" where you were comfortable, that's when complacency set it. If you don't recognize this as your condition, before you know it, 20 plus years will pass you by and you will find yourself asking *"where did the time go?"*

There is nothing worth having that doesn't come with some kind of sacrifice. You might have to stay up later, wake up earlier; be the first person to arrive and the last person to leave – maybe even for no extra pay. You don't deserve more for doing what's required of you. You deserve more for doing more, and you must establish a consistent pattern of doing more before you're rewarded for it. Done right, that pattern will transform into a habit and to do more for someone or something else, you must be willing to give *of yourself.*

Question #9:
WHY SHOULD YOU GET WHAT YOU WANT IN LIFE?

Another main reason why so many people fail to improve their circumstances and live the lives of their dreams is that they lack a reason. They don't know *why* they should live better and therefore, *how* they can go about doing it never comes to them. It was Nietzsche who said, "If you know why you can overcome any how." You see, it's not enough to just have a goal or an idea.

You have to be able to articulate *why* that goal is important to you, knowing why you should get what you want in life will serve as your fuel tank as you travel towards achieving it. And when the road gets rough – because it will get rough – knowing *why* will get you through those rough patches and turbulent times.

WHY should you make more money? Perhaps having more money will allow you to go places and do things you presently may not be able to do. Why should you spend more time with your children? Perhaps because in doing so, your children will better appreciate why you work as hard as you do when you're away. Realistically it's not enough to say, "Because I'm worth it" or "Because I deserve it." Those are empty answers. *WHY* are you worth it? *WHY* do you deserve it? Imagine you're 5 years old. What do 5 year olds ask all the time? *"WHY?!"* knowing why you should get what you want out of life will allow you to articulate it; and when you can articulate it, you can speak it into the universe and in time, manifest your outcome.

Question #10:

HOW HIGH ARE YOU WILLING TO AIM?

Michelangelo said, "People don't fail because they aim too high and miss. They fail because they aim too low and hit." It is impossible to rise above your own aspirations. Whatever you place above yourself as your cap or ceiling will be the highest you will ever go. Like the saying goes, "Your attitude will determine your altitude."

In sports they have what's called a salary cap. It is the most amount of money an organization is allowed to pay its players. But are those players bound solely by those salary caps? Are their salaries the only money they're allowed to make? Of course not. Even though many athletes make more than they can (reasonably) spend in their lifetimes – or maybe even two lifetimes, they make millions more aside from their salaries by engaging in other ventures.

Would you encourage a child to go to school and work just hard enough to make C's? Of course not. In the academic grading system, an "F" is poor or failing. A "D" is fair to poor; a "C" is average to fair, a "B" is good to fair, and an "A" is an excellent to good grade. If you had to grade yourself on where you are in your life right now, what kind of grade would you give yourself? Most people would probably give themselves an A or a B, and they would be being more generous than honest, knowing they truly deserve a C or maybe even a D. Let me ask you this... What grade are you honestly striving for?

If you're striving for a "C" and you get a "D" or an "F," whose fault is that? You see, people who just go through life trying to coast or take the easiest way out find themselves easily taken out. But if you're striving for that "A" and you get a "B," you've still proven yourself as a fighter. You're not one who is so easily taken out.

Remember what I told you not too long ago and will likely tell you again and again throughout this book... Nothing worth having comes easily. I am encouraging you to fight for that "A" lifestyle you're dreaming about. If you get it, then that will be a beautiful thing. You might not make it to that "A" lifestyle, but I can guarantee you, you won't get it shooting for a "C." As the late disc jockey, Casey Kasem used to say, "Shoot for the moon... Even if you miss you'll hit a star!"

Chapter Two
Prepare For Greatness

How many of us are happy? How many of us can pick up and go on vacation whenever we feel like it? How many of us can walk into a store and not ask "How much is it?" How many of us can walk into work on Friday and say, "I won't be coming back?" Many of us – perhaps even you – were sung the same song; "Go to school, get an education, and get a good"... what? Job - exactly. So we do just that ... We go to school. We get an education. Some of us go to and graduate from college and get that "good job." Some of us might even make really good money at that good job. But what's the trade-off? What are we giving up for that money and those benefits?

I ask the question again ... Are you happy? Are you happy when you have to miss your kids' games and recitals? Are you happy when you can't go on vacation when you want to, or you have to pick the off-seasons because it's cheaper? Are you happy having **more month left at the end of the money?!** Well, if the answer is "No," you're not happy or you're not as happy as you would like to be, then we have identified the problem in our lives. So how do we solve that problem? How do we find that missing link or key ingredient that will bring us the happiness we want?

The answer is different for each of us. The paths we have to take to get there will be different for each of us. But it's not the answer or path that will get us to where we want to be. The thing that will get us to where we want to be is our mindset. It's not the money in our pocket, the clothes on our backs or the cars parked in our driveways that define us as successful.

It's how we think. It's all about how we think. So in the pages of this book, I want to share with you some ideas that you can immediately incorporate into your lives. I want you to read and finish this book knowing that you **CAN** be happy. You **CAN** be free. You can even become wealthy! But there's a catch ... There's always a catch, right?

Well here it is ... Happiness comes at a price that may include unhappiness and discomfort. And I'll share a secret with you ... Freedom ain't free. Freedom also comes at a price. Think back to the story I shared with you about how I gained my "freedom." The cost isn't always monetary. The physical and emotional strains can sometimes make you wish you could just throw some money at your troubles to make them go away. But no, some things you just have to **work** through.

Now, I am not here to try and change your way of thinking - just add on to it. But if you discover where you might be off course and these words change your thinking, I won't be mad either. I am not here to tell you that whatever you've been doing is wrong. In fact, I'll go so far as to say you don't have to believe a word I say!

You see, I'm only speaking from my own experiences. The ideas and insights I'm sharing with you are a reflection of my results and those of the people whom I've studied, met and spoken with. My only goal is to share with you some ideas that have worked for me and others, and afford you the opportunity to incorporate those ideas into your life. Should any changes be made in your lives they will be changes that you decide to make based on what best fits your circumstances.

Look at it like this ... Take this time to imagine yourself shopping for clothes. Out of everything I'm saying, take what fits for you and discard the rest. I'm here to talk to you today about becoming successful. In this chapter,

I'm going to share with you two things:
1. Three of the most important tools you will need in order to have the proper mindset in order to become successful in whatever you to strive to accomplish; and,
2. A simple 5-step plan to get you started.

So let's get started...

PURPOSE, PREPARATION & PERSEVERANCE

Contrary to what many people may believe, there is no cookie-cutter recipe to becoming successful. There is no one book that will guarantee anyone success, any more than there is just one outfit you can wear that will go with every mood you have and every environment you're in. The reason for this is because there are as many different views of success as there are people on the planet. For some people being successful is having the bills paid. For others it might be reaching a certain level or position at their job; and yet for many others it may be acquiring certain status symbols such as cars, clothes, and jewelry.

For me, success is a combination of all those things, but more importantly, it is the acquisition of wisdom along this journey called life. You see, there are all kinds of twists and turns that we encounter on our journeys; some lead us where we want to be and others show us where we don't want to be.

The first step to becoming successful is taking accountability for your flaws as well as your successes. I believe that in order to know where we want to be, we have to know exactly where we are. We have to take stock of ourselves and in doing so we have to be very honest with ourselves ... I mean brutally honest with ourselves, because when you are brutally honest with yourself and acknowledge where your flaws are, it's easier for you to begin self-correcting and you make it more difficult for others to have grounds to criticize you. But we'll talk about such people in a few minutes.

What I want to get across to you are some of the things necessary to take your lives to the next level, and after hearing some of these things you might even go so far as to say, **"But Harold** (that's what the "H" in "H.S. Reed, Jr." stands for), **that's common sense,"** and you could very well be right; however, allow me share with you my view on "common sense" ... If common sense were "common," everyone would have it, and we all **know** that not to always be the case. I'm going to share with you some tools that will help you in finding your way. These tools are not unknown to the masses, but by far and large, they are **unused** by the masses.

You see, people who achieve what they consider to be their own definitions of success don't see their journeys as minefields that are impossible to pass through. They see their journeys as minefields where whatever they have set as a goal is on the other side. They anticipate the trips and pitfalls. They know they just have to find a way to successfully navigate around them until they get to the other side. So, the first tool you're going to need to use on your journey is...

Purpose

Again, it was Nietzsche who said, "He who has a why can endure any 'how.'" One of the many things that keep people from finding the success they claim to want is that their focus is off. They may see the goal they want to set for themselves, but they focus more on "how" they're going to achieve it than "why" they want to achieve the goal, and because they don't know why they want to achieve their goals, they fall victim to the obstacles in their path and give up.

When you know why you're doing something, it becomes easier to do because it makes sense. For example, growing up, what was the one question you asked your parents that would guarantee you the answer, "Because I said so"? ... "WHY?!"

As we got older our childhood curiosity wavered. As we got older we learned more, therefore we knew more, and for many of us, we reach a point in our lives when we believe we **know everything** we think we need to know. As we got older we became more self-sufficient; and in becoming self-sufficient we learned "how" to do things on our own. So when it comes down to getting something done we tend to focus on how we're going to get it done, and figure that the "why" is simply because either "we have to" or it will otherwise work itself out along the way.

Moving forward, ***define your purpose.*** Go back to asking "Why?" You see, success doesn't come from having the right answers. It comes from asking the right questions. Without questions there are no answers. Now you can ask all kinds of questions to all kinds of people, but the best way to define your purpose and determine what will work best for you is for you to ask those questions to yourself.

When you ask yourself why something is important to you, your mind begins coming up with answers. Some of those answers might be wrong, but some of those answers will be right – and you will find your way.

Ask yourself "Why do I want to have or become this thing?" At this stage in the process the only "how" that matters is NOT "How do I?" but *"How does having or being this thing improve my life?"* Once you've defined and determined your purpose, you can begin the next logical step in your journey or process, which is...

Preparation

In 1992, I was taught a lesson in preparation that continues to pay off to this very day every time I use it. That lesson was called *"the 7P's,"* which stands for *"Proper Pre-Planning Prevents Piss-Poor Performance."* A lot of the time people get a halfway decent idea in their head and just go off half-cocked to see it to fruition. Sometimes it works out for them. Most times it doesn't.

When I learned "the 7P's" I was going through the process of pledging Groove Phi Groove Social Fellowship Incorporated®. During that process, I was faced with various tasks. Knowing what was expected of me, I would prepare for the assignments I had to accomplish and then go so far as to anticipate what would logically come next and be prepared for that as well. It was kind of like reading a chapter in a book for a homework assignment and then reading the next chapter ahead of time.

When you go about setting goals and striving to be more than what you are, you have to know what you're getting yourself into. This is where – after you've determined your "Why" by defining your purpose – you begin formulating your "How." One thing you have to realize is that there are a variety of ways to achieve your goals. As I said earlier, there's no cookie-cutter recipe to becoming successful. However, at the same time, people need to realize that what worked for someone else might not work for them.

We all have different experiences and different ways of viewing and reacting to things and because of this there is no guarantee that because "ABC" worked for me, it's going to work for you. This is why I suggest you take what fits and discard the rest.

Also ... When preparing for your greatness, you have to really take a cold, hard and solid look at how you react to things. You might have to do some studying and strategizing. You might have to create some contingency plans. Now, I have heard people say that they never had a "Plan B" because they put all of their faith in their "Plan A," and if that works for them – God bless them ... but remember ... not everything works the same way for everybody.

Personally, I believe in having as many available options as possible. Now, if you can get it all done with "Plan A" cool; but if there's a hitch in the giddy-up, you're going to feel glad knowing that you can pop the clutch and shift right into 2nd or 3rd gear as necessary!

In the words of the Civil Rights leader, Whitney M. Young, *"It is better to be prepared for an opportunity and not have one than to have an opportunity and not be prepared."*

Most people believe that in some way successful people are lucky, and believe that success is some random occurrence that walks hand in hand with luck. However, I subscribe to the definition of luck as penned by the Roman philosopher, Seneca, who said, *"Luck is what happens when preparation meets opportunity."* Finally, the next tool you're going to need is...

Perseverance

As I shared with you earlier, there's an old saying that goes, "If you want to hear God laugh, tell Him what you've got planned." There's another saying that goes, "The best plans of mice and men often go awry;" and yet a third saying that goes, "God may not come when you call but He's always on time!"

True and lasting success does not always come when you want it to come. I always tell people that the obstacles we face are God's way of testing us – testing our worthiness to have that which we are striving for. Just because you want something does not automatically entitle you to have it. You can spew all of the affirmations in the world, but if you're not out there putting in the necessary work, it's not going to happen – and whatever measure of what you think is success you achieved by taking shortcuts – it's only a fraction of what you're truly capable of receiving by going all out for the long haul.

I believe that people are conditioned to think that achieving a particular goal is supposed to take a given amount of time; and for many things this is true, but if you're setting out to break new ground and venture into uncharted territory, who's to say how long it may take? It's supposed to take 4 years to get through college, but how many people do we know took 5 or 6 years to graduate? Counting the years between the time I dropped out of college and went back to earn my degree, it took me about 25 years!

Why might it take one person 5, 6, or even 25 years to graduate college, or reach a certain position on their job, or even make a million dollars? It has a lot to do with circumstances. We all have different circumstances that affect our lives in many different ways. The problem is that people tend to judge other people's moves and outcomes through their own circumstances and personal values.

However, regardless of our means – the money we make to survive and function – we all have to live within our own sphere of circumstances and values, and we have to understand that our proverbial ship will come in when it is supposed to come in, and not a single day sooner. The best thing – the most important thing we have to do is continue to grind and put in the necessary work until the rewards we are due are bestowed upon us.

You have to keep the faith and stay focused and persistent towards achieving your goal. The basketball courts in city playgrounds all over the country are chock full of men and women with broken dreams of making it big, as are the night-clubs, street corners, and any other place you can think of where there are people who had big dreams ... and little perseverance.

The "5 STAR SUCCESS PLAN"

So how do you get started? What steps must you take towards heading in the right direction? Well ... I'd like to share with you what I call my **"5 Star Success Plan."** I developed this plan from years of studying successful people in a variety of disciplines.

1. DETERMINE YOUR GOAL

Success does not come like it does in the fairy tales. By that I mean it does not go in the order of "Once upon a time" leading up to "and they lived happily ever after." In real life, if you want to succeed you have to see the success and then work backwards.

Another way of "seeing the success" is to determine your goal. You must be clear about what it is that you are setting out to accomplish. Envision what your life will be like once you've accomplished your goal. Be specific. What are the sights and smells you expect to experience? How will you carry yourself around people once you've achieved your goal? How will they carry themselves around you?

Quick story ... When I started my career in Law Enforcement I was making about $40K a year. My level of contact and conversation with my superiors was relegated to the work at hand. I was either submitting reports or briefing them on what happened at the scene of a particular incident. Two years into my career, I was hired by another agency in another town and the job came with a **_significant_** bump-up in pay. About a year and a half later, I ran into one of the Captains from my old agency who happened to live in the town where I had begun working.

What's funny was **_he was the one who came up to me and initiated a conversation!_** I can literally count on one hand how many times I spoke with him when he was my superior officer – and still have a couple fingers to spare! During the conversation, he asked politely asked me how much money I was making on my new job – which at that time was about $75K a year.

He winced, because he knew that my salary as a Patrolman at my new agency was roughly close to the rank of Lieutenant at my former department where he still worked. Salary-wise, I was **_close_** to where he was and maybe a year or two away from catching up to him! After that conversation, whenever I saw him around town, it was "Hey Harold! How ya doin' buddy? How's the family?!"

So know that when you achieve your goals, whether you change in one way or another or not, I can guarantee you that there will be some people around you who will change – at least how they act around you.

Okay, let's get back on track. What you will find is that the more you focus on these elements; envisioning what life will be like after having achieved your goal, the more your mind will work to seek out to the means to manifesting those elements in order satisfy the disconnect between the perceived experience and the actual experience. By determining your goal, you begin setting yourself up for success because you have established what living in your success will be like.

2. CREATE YOUR TEAM

One of the wealthiest men in American history, Andrew Carnegie owed the acquisition of his wealth to the team he built. He called his team "the Master Mind," which he defined as, "An alliance of two or more minds, working together in the spirit of perfect harmony, for the attainment of a definite purpose."

No one person totally succeeds on his or her own. Steve Jobs didn't create and build Apple on his own. He had a partner named Steve Wozniak. Bill Gates didn't create and build Microsoft by himself; he had a partner named Paul Allen; and Mark Zuckerberg started Facebook with three partners - Eduardo Saverin, Dustin Moskovitz and Chris Hughes.

These men have changed the world, and while in each of these particular entities there may be one man's name who stands above the others; neither Apple, Microsoft nor Facebook would be what they are were it not for those lesser known team players who were there from the start.

If you are going to succeed in any given endeavor, you need to surround yourself with quality like-minded people. It's a good thing if you can create a team with friends, but that can be a dangerous game if you're not all on the same page from the start. Be careful who you approach and share your vision with.

A particular friend might be good to hang with when it comes to watching a game, shooting hoops, going out to the club or shopping, but that does not mean they would be a good fit for your business or that they would even be willing to share in your vision.

In creating your team, you have to really have to define the nature of the relationships between you and the prospective members of that team. Friendships can exist within the team construct, but only for as long as everyone is working in harmony. Differences will always arise, but you have to be able to work through those differences for the benefit of the team's overall goals.

Also in creating your team, everyone has to bring something to the table. Everyone has to serve a significant and valuable function. This way, no one can be accused of just going along for the ride. You may have the overall vision, but not all of the resources to pull it off. You will need people on your team who can compensate for what you and other members lack to pull off an overall collective result.

3. <u>DEVISE YOUR PLAN</u>

As I said earlier, success does not come from having the right answers. It comes from asking the right questions. In devising your plan, you've already established what your goal is. The only riddle is getting there. Solve the riddles and you win the prize! Begin asking questions ... What is it going to take to achieve your goals? How much will it cost? Where will the money come from? What resources will you need? What resources do you have at your disposal? What resources do your team members have? What resources can they acquire? How long will it take you to achieve your goal?

These are but a few examples of the types of questions you will have to ask of yourself and your team as you begin the process of achieving your goals. Having a goal is not enough. You have to have a plan to achieve it. Answering those questions, and any others that are pertinent to the achievement of your goal will help you in devising your plan.

4. <u>UNIFY YOUR RESOURCES</u>

This is why you create a team. No one person can do it on his or her own - and why should they? With everyone on the team bringing their skills to the collective, the team comes closer to achieving its goal. One person might be good with numbers; another computers; someone else might be great with people and be a great networker, and yet someone else who is good with organizing and prioritizing.

This is where steps 2 and 3 come into play and why they are so important. Everyone on the team has to bring something of value to the collective. It can be something as simple as everyone chipping in for dinner or building a multi-million dollar business. When everyone shares their resources to benefit of the common good and the common goal, everyone benefits. You actually increase your personal power by however many people are on your team. Imagine your fight to succeed as a game of Tug of War. You can pull the rope alone or you can use the strength of four or five people to pull it.

If you're more of a people-person than your teammates, you might be the mouthpiece of the team. Another member might be a wiz at graphic design or marketing and advertising, and yet another might see the value in the vision, but the only value he or she may bring to the table is the money to invest in the goal. Everyone must bring *something* to the table. No one rides for free! That's the difference between having a team and having an entourage.

5. TAKE ACTION

Nothing happens unless and until you take action. You can draw up all the plans and strategies you can think of. You can build a team of five people or you can recruit an army of followers; however, in order for people to "follow" you, you have to be going somewhere. And in order for you to go anywhere, you have to take action.

It is believed by many that taking action is the hardest step in this process. What's ironic about this being the last item on the list is that even though the command to "TAKE ACTION" may seem intimidating, if you've already taken steps 2, 3, & 4, you've already begun taking step 5.

It takes action to *"Devise Your Plan"* because you may have to do all kinds of research to validate the worth of achieving your goal. It takes action to *"Create Your Team"* because you now have to actually approach people, share your vision with them and hope they see the value in it and are willing to join your team. And it takes action to *"Unify Your Resources"* because when it comes time for the team members to put their talents and skills to use, that's truly when the rubber meets the road.

But that is why *"Take Action"* is actually listed as the last step in this process. It's the kick in your pants you need to really get started. It "takes action" to build a rocket ship or a fast car; however, once that rocket ship or car has been built what is it going to take to actually see if it works? ACTION... Someone is going to have to get in, turn the key and step on the gas. Otherwise how else are you going to know if the goal you determined is actually attainable?

How else are you going to know if you have the right people on your team? How else are you going to know if your plan was on point or flawed at some point? How else are you going to know if you had enough resources ... unless you take action?

So let's sum this up...

1. DETERMINE YOUR GOAL - What are you setting out to accomplish?

2. CREATE YOUR TEAM - Who is going to help you accomplish it?

3. DEVISE YOUR PLAN - How are you going to accomplish it?

4. UNIFY YOUR RESOURCES - What do you have at your disposal to accomplish it?

5. TAKE ACTION - Get to work.

Yes ... The plan really is just that simple. Wait a minute ... As you're reading this page, I'm now reading your mind. You're thinking, *"Well, Harold, that's easier said than done."* And you know what? *YOU'RE RIGHT!* The plan is simple but the complexity comes into play in the implementation of the plan. People want simplicity, but simplicity comes at a price, and like it or not, complexity is that price. People want success, but the price to pay in succeeding is overcoming all of the obstacles that stand in your way. This plan is but another tool to help in overcoming those obstacles.

There is no such thing as an "overnight success," at least not in the sense that one day somebody was nobody, went to bed that night, and then woke up the next day to be Michael Jordan, Oprah Winfrey, Tyler Perry, Beyoncé or Barack Obama. These people, and those who have achieved what they define as their own levels of success did so through long tedious work.

Winning the lottery doesn't make you successful. It doesn't even make you wealthy. It simply makes you rich, and the reality is you will hear a lot more stories about people who went from rags to riches, only to go back to rags. However, the stories you'll hear about people going from wealthy to washed-out are fewer and far between. Preparing for your greatness will prepare you for how to live once you've achieved it. The work will be what makes you appreciate all that you've gained.

It will be all of the struggles you endured; all of the nights you stayed up 3-4 hours later, all of the mornings you woke up 3-4 hours earlier; the money you lost, the money you made back only to lose again; the people who you trusted who turned out to be snakes; all of the broken promises and deals that were guaranteed only to fall through at the last minute. These are the things you must prepare for in the process of receiving and being able to live in your greatness.

Chapter Three
Wealth is Something in
Never-Ending Abundance

One of the most difficult things to make people understand is that there is more than enough of everything for everyone. The problem, as I see it, is that because people see something as out of reach, they think it's not theirs to have. Actually, when people see something as out of reach, one of three things happens:

1. They reach out anyway and get what they want;
2. They reach out, don't get what they want, and never attempt to reach again.
3. They look, but never reach at all.

Those who reach out and get what they want are the ones who actually go all out to get what they want. The reaching is nothing more than putting in the required work to achieve the desired results. These people are vastly outnumbered by people in the other two categories.

Those who reach out; don't get what they want, and never attempt to reach again are the people who give up on what they're reaching for when they face any signs of adversity while they were reaching. Either no one told them that there would be rough patches along the way, or they just knew they were special enough or cute enough or connected enough to where they could just bypass those rough patches. These people feel as though they're above earning what they're yearning, which is why they never get what they want.

And then there are those who never reach at all and these people are the saddest. These are the people who have resigned themselves to accepting their circumstances because they don't believe they are supposed to have more. Their entire existence becomes one huge comfort zone.

Now if you are friends with people like this, guess what? You live inside of their comfort zone. You may have never asked to be there, but there you are. Now ... as long as you don't rock the boat and you just go with the flow there aren't any problems. However, if you decide that you want more out of your life, that's when all hell is going to break loose because when you see yourself having more and go about doing more, that friend of yours sees less in him- or herself, and you become a threat to their comfort zone.

These are the people who believe that not everyone can be wealthy, but the fact of the matter is this ... Everyone could become wealthy if they were willing to learn and follow the rules to acquire wealth. So, it's not that everyone can't become wealthy because there's not enough wealth in the world. The reality is everyone won't become wealthy because not everyone is willing to do what's required to become wealthy.

So what's required of us to become wealthy? **MORE**. We have to be willing to do more. How much? **MORE**. How much more? As much more as it takes to achieve your goal. Now, what exactly do you have to do? That depends on what you want to accomplish. The one thing I can guarantee you is that it's going to take time, and that is where people begin to lose hope. People begin to lose hope because they're impatient, and when what they want to have doesn't come as quickly as they dreamed it would, they don't see it happening at all.

When people don't see something as possible for themselves, they don't see it as being possible for anyone. Yet and still, people all over the world become wealthy every day. You see, just because the world stops spinning for you, doesn't mean it stops spinning. You might quit, but the next person won't.

All it takes is the right idea or the right product or service, to reach the right person at the right time. You may have no control over who the right person is. You may have even less control over when the right time is, but if you've got the right idea, the right product and or the right service, you've got 40%-60% of the problem solved.

Many of the reasons why so many people do not have as much as they could have in this life are the false beliefs that:
1. There is not enough wealth in the world for them to have more of what they want;
2. They weren't born with the right last name;

3. They weren't born in the right zip code, or the people who do have more are just hoarding it all and keeping everyone else from having more.

Here's the thing. These beliefs are both 100% true and 100% crap depending on what you believe. If you believe that there's not enough wealth in the world for you to have some of it, then you will never be inspired to go after any of it. You'll just be stuck with whatever is left over. It was Abraham Lincoln who said *"Good things may come to those who wait, but only the things left behind by those who hustle."*

On the other hand, if you believe that there's a million dollars somewhere out there with your name on it, all you have to do is find it. And guess what? That's going to take some work. So you see ... the reality is not that there isn't enough wealth to go around. The reality is that there are not enough people who are willing to work for it.

In 2011, the "Occupy Wall Street" protest movement created new buzzwords like "the 99%" and the "1%." Well, for years I have said that 90% of the world's wealth is owned by 10% of the population. I'll even take it a couple steps further. Now I'm certain that at SOME point in your life you've watched television.

Roughly guessing ... the average cast of a sitcom or drama seen on any given weeknight is somewhere between 5 to 8 people, but with over 90% of the population either owning or having access to a television set, it's safe to say that there are more people watching TV than there are people **on** TV, right? Yet when you turn off that TV, who has more money in the bank, the watchers or the performers? **The performers.** I submit to you that successful people will **always** be in the minority because successful people are always the ones who are willing to **do more**.

When you watch a play or a concert or even listen to a new CD, you're witnessing a one-time event; and if performed well, it may be a flawless performance. What you **don't** see are the countless hours of practice they put in. Any successful person will tell you that it takes years of hard work in order to become an "overnight sensation."

In a world where the spending power of African American's - if measured as a country would place us as the 16th wealthiest country ... In a world where the spending power of the African American community is set to be upwards of $1.1 Trillion dollars by 2015 ... I submit to you that there is more wealth in the world than we know what to do with. It's just unfocused collectively.

I submit to you that when you make the time to take the time to learn what to do with some of it, you'll eventually get your piece of it. I submit to you that you can have what you want and you can be what you want ... provided you are willing to do what will be required of you. There is more than enough wealth for all of us to have some because there will always be those who quit and give up on their dreams. As long as you provide quality and value, you will get your share.

Chapter Four
Consumers vs. Contributors

Why is it so hard for people to follow their dreams? Well, let's first take a look at where dreams come from. Our dreams are the movies of our subconscious minds where we can either be the stars or the victims. When you're the hero, you're the star. When you're being chased by the zombies or aliens, you're the victim. One thing is certain... regardless of if you're the star or the victim in your dreams; you have the power to transform your dreams into your reality.

So in looking into why it is so hard for people to follow their dreams; and understanding that our dreams are products of the intangibility of our subconscious, then the problem must exist in a person's lack of belief in that they have the power to make something out of nothing. These are the people who are life's **consumers**. These are the people who suffer from what I call "L.T.N.P.D.I. syndrome." "L.T.N.P.D.I." stands for *"let the next person do it."* Those who suffer from "let the next person do it" syndrome believe that everything short of (or perhaps including) paying their bills is **someone else's** job.

It's **someone else's** job to teach their children. It's someone else's job to catch criminals and put out fires. It's **someone else's** job to make sure government runs the way it's supposed to. Likewise, when the things that were **someone else's** job to do go wrong then naturally it's someone else's fault. Strangely, even though it's **someone else's** job to do all of these things when things go wrong in the lives of those suffering from "let the next person do it" syndrome that she was **someone else's** fault.

It's *someone else's* fault when their children don't do well in school – even though they allowed their children to spend more time mastering video games than studying. It was *someone else's* fault when their car got broken into – despite the fact that they were the ones who left their $1,000 golf clubs sitting in the back seat. And it was *someone else's* fault when the councilperson (who got elected because certain people didn't bother to go out and vote) got caught with his/her hand in the cookie jar.

"Someone else" has a lot of responsibility, and *"someone else"* is the cause of a lot of trouble in people's lives; however, *"someone else"* is rarely the one with whom these people share the credit with when things tend to go good in their lives.

I firmly believe that 90% of the world's wealth is owned by 10% of the world's population. I will go even further suspect that the 10% of the world's population that owns 90% of the world's wealth are the same people that those "L.T.N.P.D.I." folks refer to as *"someone else."*

So, as I said earlier, these people who are suffering from "L.T.N.P.D.I." syndrome are life's consumers. They are the 90% of the people who have no ownership in any of the world's wealth. If you haven't guessed by now, the name I give to that other 10%; well, those people are life's contributors.

There are all kinds of people in this world. Here, I am going to discuss two very significant ones... **consumers and contributors.** One of the many ebbs and flows in the circle of life revolve around the concept of give and take. In examining the idea or belief that 90% of the world's wealth is owned by 10% of the world's population, I find myself also believing and I submit to you that the 10% who are wealth owners of the world are in one form or another life's contributors while the remaining 90% of the people are the consumers.

Literally speaking, contributors contribute; meaning they give or provide, whereas consumers consume - meaning they take or acquire. Personally, I believe in a generous God. I believe the universe in which we live is just fertile and full of opportunity as the ocean is full of fish. When a fisherman goes out into the water, how many fish do you think you'll catch if he puts nothing on his hook before casting his line?

Right... few if any at all in order for that fisherman to reap the rewards he seeks from the water he must "contribute" something. Without contributing what's necessary to attract the fish, he is nothing more than a consumer who wants to take without giving. On the flipside, take a look at those fish. They want nothing to do with an empty hook, but if there's something tasty enough of them to "consume," the actually end up "contributing" their own lives. You see, you can't go through life just taking. At some point the scales will have to be balanced and you **will** have to make some kind of contribution.

Zig Ziglar often said you can have everything you want in life by helping other people get what they want. What he was telling us is that we are all capable of living out our dreams (the consumer side) as long as we help other people realize theirs (the contributor side).

One of the biggest misconceptions is that rich get richer at the expense of the poor. Granted, there are people who have an abundance of money and are scrupulously impoverished, but do believe that such people are the exception and not the rule. You see, the truth is there are a plethora of millionaires who lead humble and quiet lives. One of the secrets to their success and wealth... generosity.

Some call it charity, giving, tithing... me... I call it contributing. You see, consuming and contributing are two sides of the same coin. We all possess the ability to do one more than the other, but certainly none of us can go through life doing neither.

There will always be more consumers than there are contributors. There will always be more people who want to "Let The Next Person Do It." This is not being negative – oh no ... this is just calling it straight down the middle. The reason why there will always be a vast majority of consumers over contributors is because; although it is better to give than receive, it is also harder to give than it is to receive.

Now, it is just a matter of natural fact that those who go the extra mile and stay true to themselves, their dreams, and their goals are the ones who ultimately succeed. Those who take the easy way out time after time, eventually find themselves as such... **_OUT. Out_** of the game, **_out_** of opportunities, **_out_** of luck, and ultimately **_out of time!_**

Contributors will always be in the minority because there are only a select few (10%) who understand that the reason why it is better to give than it is to receive is because the more you give, the more you get. The more people you help out in the world, the more people out in the world will find a way to help you. People want to be part of a good thing. Some people just want to get on board for the high times -- these are the consumers; they want to gain something via association.

On the other hand, there are also people who want to be a part of a good thing because it **_IS_** a good thing and they wish to contribute their time, effort, energy, and maybe even money to make that good thing a better thing.

What I want you to understand is the difference between consumers and contributors is not about contrasting unsuccessful people against successful people. It's not about condemning 90% of the world's population to not owning a portion of that 90% of the world's wealth.

ABSOULUTELY NOT! What I want you to understand is that the difference between being a consumer and a contributor bears a direct reflection on your ability to take your dreams and convert them into your reality.

By becoming a contributor; by giving of yourself, by drawing from the well of good will that exists within you, God takes notice – and when God takes notice He begins to draw from that abundant ocean called the Universe and He rains His blessings down upon you.

By becoming a contributor and giving of yourself, you will find that you will not be or go without. Even when the times get tough – *especially* when the times get tough, God will make his presence known in your life. You'll find an extra and unexpected $20 bill in your pants pocket. Your boss might call out sick on a day when you might not feel like dealing with him or her. Investors may make themselves known to back your idea or invention.

By becoming a contributor it becomes more and more difficult to become or ever really be a consumer. You see, the things that contributors receive beyond their means for living are the rewards they deserve for the service they provide. It was the late congresswoman, Shirley Chisolm, who said, *"Service is the rent we pay for the privilege of living on this earth."* This is a woman who epitomized what it means to be a contributor, becoming the first African American woman elected to Congress and to run for the office of President of the United States.

Finally, being a contributor is not about giving a couple of tax-deductible charitable contributions, or giving with the hopes of catching some huge windfall or payback. God is watching and He knows your heart better than you do. Granted, I did state earlier that many of the world's wealthiest people owe their wealth in some part to their generosity. However, you've got to be a giver – a contributor; if for no other reason, because it's the right thing to do.

Some of the world's greatest contributors of our time were not people of wealthy means. Mahatma Gandhi, Mother Theresa, Dr. Martin Luther King, Jr. ... none of these people were measured by their bank accounts. In fact, by all measures of material wealth, these people would range from poor to middle-class; however, no one can deny that these people changed the world by all they contributed and gave of themselves.. There are great rewards for being a contributor more than being a consumer, but never forget ... *to whom much is given much is required.*

Chapter Five
H.E.R.O.

Now, I would like to talk to you about heroes. When I was a kid, heroes could fly, climb walls, swing from ropes and could fight bad guy after bad guy after bad guy. And no matter how much of a beating they may have taken they would always get back up and fight even harder.

But despite all of the cartoons and comic books, my most favorite hero was and is ... my father. Even though I was kind of shy as kid, my father taught me how not to allow myself to be bullied. My father taught me the value of hard work; the value of a dollar, and he taught me how to go after what I want in life. Ultimately, my father taught me how to be a man.

Sadly far too many young people don't have that man in their lives to either teach our boys how to be men or our daughters what to look for in a man. I'm only one man, and I already have two boys of my own, but I believe in the African adage, "it takes a village to raise a child." I believe that It's my responsibility to be an example of what a good man is, and be that example for as many young people that need it. Having said that, I make myself available to mentor, motivate and encourage every group of young people I speak to.

Now let's continue. Let me ask you a question ... What is a hero to you?

Let me tell you what a hero is to me. To me, *"H.E.R.O."* is an acronym which stands for *"Human Excellence Repeated Over."* To me a hero is not only someone who does great things, but someone who does great things over and over again; and someone who does great things over and over again is giving you an example of how to better yourself. Someone who is doing great things over and over again is giving you an example of what it means to go through the ups and downs of life and still come out on top.

And don't get it twisted ... there *are* going to be downs in your lives. Every day is not going to be a sunny day. You see ... It's not the high times or the "up" times that make people heroes. Heroes have to overcome. Heroes have to go through some things. This is why they say "You can't have a testimony unless you've passed the test, and you can't have a message unless you done been through some mess."

So ... Having passed my tests and having been through some mess, I'm going to share just two lessons with you that you can use to become heroes yourselves. The first lesson comes from a man named Jim Rohn. He's another one of my heroes and from him I learned and am now going to share with you *"The Ant Philosophy."*

1. ANTS NEVER QUIT.

If they're headed somewhere and you try to stop them, they'll look for another way. They'll climb over, they'll crawl under, they'll climb around ... they will keep looking for another way.   So the lesson here is, NEVER quit looking for a way to get to where you're supposed to go.

2. ANTS THINK "WINTER" ALL SUMMER LONG.

You can't think "nice" when it's nice. You've got to be prepared for when it's not nice. In the summer, you've got to think storm – You've got to think rock. You can't think sandy beaches and sun. You've got to be prepared for those down times.

3. ANTS THINK "SUMMER" ALL WINTER LONG.

Through the cold of winter, ants must be thinking, "This won't last long ... We'll soon be out of here." After having prepared for the winter, when winter comes, you're good. When those down times I was telling you about come; and they will always come, you're warm. You've got shelter. You've got food. Even though you've got to endure those down times, you know that there's a light at the end of the tunnel. You must believe that summer will come around again.

4. HOW MUCH WILL AN ANT GATHER DURING TIIE SUMMER TO PREPARE FOR THE WINTER?

All he possibly can! The lesson to be learned from ants here is for you to do all you can to prepare yourself for the hard times and to prepare yourself to be great!

Now ... If you never knew before, let me tell you now that as you get older, there are going to be obstacles. People are going to stand in your way. People are going to talk about you behind your back - and in your face. People are going to tell you what you can't do. There will be dark days and cold nights ... So now you know.

However, when those times come ... When you realize you're dealing with those kinds of people, remember those ants! Remember that ants never quit. Remember that when things are nice and smooth, they're preparing for when the road is going to get rough, and when the road does get rough, they know it won't last forever. And here's the thing, ants aren't going to be too worried about the down times because they've done everything they could to be prepared the whole time.

The second lesson I want to teach you is that you have what it takes to be a *"H.E.R.O."* you have what it takes to be an example of *"Human Excellence Repeated Over."* But there's a secret to it, and here it is ... You just have to believe in yourself and do great things over and over again. Right now (if you're a teen or college student), hopefully, the most you should really have to worry about is doing well in school, so if you're getting those A's on your report cards, those are the great things you need to be doing over and over again.

If you're out there in the workforce, you may have a few more balls being juggled, a few additional plates spinning. Regardless of whether you're young, old; or some happy place in between, you must realize – as businessman A.L. Williams said, "All you can do is all you can do, but all you can do is enough."

Say this to yourself right now ... "A job well done ... Is its own reward."

You have to be your biggest cheerleader. You have to know that when you do good things, or just the right thing, the reward is not in the gifts or the pats on the back. The reward is in knowing you did what was right. Because – let me tell you – there are going to be times in your life when you do something great that no one will pay attention to. There are going to be times when you will help people and they will say everything **but** "Thank You."

Does that mean you stop doing those great things? Does that mean you stop helping people and doing what's right? As long as you can look at what you've done and say, "I did a good thing," trust me when I tell you that that's all you will ever need. So if you do something great and other people recognize and applaud you that's a bonus. That's extra. The last lesson I want to teach you is that *success has no age limit.*

There's nothing stopping you from being a success right where you are, just as old as you are right now. In Atlanta, Georgia there is a young man named Stephen Stafford, who at 16 years old was taking advanced classes at Morehouse College. He started going to Morehouse when he was 13. There's another young man named Dr. Farrah Gray.

Dr. Gray was born and raised in the projects of Chicago, who became a self-made millionaire at the age of 14. Colonel Harland Sanders did not succeed with his fried chicken recipe until he was in his 70's. Remember that the next time you're eating a piece of KFC (Kentucky Fried Chicken).

What dreams or talents do you have that, if you really applied yourself, could improve your lives and the lives of those you love? Don't just watch these other people doing great things over and over … **BECOME ONE OF THEM!** Discover what makes you happy. Discover what you can do and do well … then **DO IT AND DO IT WELL.**

Remember "The Ant Philosophy" and never give up. Remember that you are great because **YOU SAY SO.** Remember that success has no age limit, and I guarantee you that if you keep doing these great things over and over again that you will someday become an example of *"Human Excellence Repeated Over"* … I guarantee you that someday there will be someone who will look at you and say … **YOU ARE MY HERO!**

Chapter Six
Making a Difference

You, and every other person born into this world; no matter how old you are, no matter where you are in life, no matter how much money or education you have – or don't have, were born with certain gifts and talents you can use to make a difference. Sadly, too many people get caught up and eventually stuck in what Zig Ziglar called "stinkin' thinkin'."

Stinkin' thinkin' is believing that where you came from determines where you should end up. Stinkin' thinkin' is believing that because you were born into a family that did not have money and education that these are things you can't have for yourself. In short, stinkin' thinkin' is any line of thought that you allow to convince yourself that you can't improve your condition.

Stinkin' thinkin' is convincing yourself to quit just because the road gets rough, and stinkin' thinkin' is expecting everything you try to be easy, only to quit when you discover that it's not. Stinkin' thinkin' allows you to succeed at only one thing... Failure. And if you want to make a difference, the first thing you have to do is rid yourself of any stinkin' thinkin'.

Early in my law enforcement career, I allowed stinkin' thinkin' to jerk me out of what could've been a great opportunity. I was on the job for less than a year, but I was able to get myself an interview with the chief investigator of the Middlesex County Prosecutor's Office. During my interview, the chief asked me "Harold, do you have any experience with undercover investigations?" "No sir," was my answer to that question and just about every "experience" related question he asked.

I walked out of his office crushed. I felt totally inadequate and unqualified, and I allowed stinkin' thinkin' to take over. Stinkin' thinkin' had me saying to myself "What do you think you are trying to do making that kind of move? You ain't ready for that job. You're only going to embarrass yourself." So I wrote the chief a letter thanking him for his time, and telling him I thought it best if I stayed where I was and got more of that "experience" he was asking me about, and I withdrew myself from his consideration.

About a week or two later I got a phone call from my friend Stan. Now Stan and I were security guards together and he started out as a New Jersey Transit cop, but got hired by and had been working at the Prosecutor's Office for couple of years. So Stan called me and said, "Dude, what did you do?" He said, "Dude, the chief told me you pulled out." I said, "Man, I sat in that office and felt like a fool. Everything he asked me about I had no experience in." Then Stan said, "Dude, that's exactly why he was going to hire you. You were the perfect candidate. Not having much experience meant that you didn't have any bad habits to be broken out of."

I never thought about it like that. So I reached out to the chief asked for a second meeting, which he gave me. However it was truly a courtesy. I never did get a second chance. It's true when they say you never get a second chance to make a first impression, and while I did make a good first impression in that first interview, that letter ruined it all. It cast a cloud over me that said I was indecisive, and I swore that I would never allow indecisiveness to plague me again if ever I had another opportunity like that.

A few months later I did get another opportunity. I was introduced to Jim McGreevy when he was running for governor of New Jersey. He arranged a meeting for me with the Deputy Chief of Police of Woodbridge Township where he was the mayor at the time. At that meeting, I was interviewed by both the Deputy Chief and the Chief of Police.

They asked me many of the same questions that the Prosecutor's Office had asked. By this time, however, I was a little more seasoned and they offered me a job under two conditions: (1) I move to Woodbridge and become a resident there within six months and (2) the department I was with had to approve the transfer.

The moving part was easy. My wife, Taria, and I were engaged at the time, planning our wedding and were looking for a place to live that wasn't far from either of our parents, and Woodbridge was practically in the middle of them both. So we got ourselves an apartment there and got married a few months later. However by the end of the six months, my department rejected the transfer request.

So guess who showed up again? Stinkin' thinkin'! That voice in my head came back saying, "Did you really think you were going to get that job? There are guys here with 10 years' experience or more trying to go to other departments. You've only been here for two years you think they're going to let **you** go?" And I remember saying "**SHUT UP!** I don't care about those guys!" So I wrote the Chief of Police a letter letting him know that my transfer request was rejected, but I also told him "don't forget my name because you're going to be hearing from me again."

The next year I took the Civil Service exam and almost 2 months to the day after the birth of my first son they called me and told me I was number three on the hiring list and the job was mine if I wanted it. So don't allow stinkin' thinkin' to stand in your way! When you have those thoughts come into your head and you hear that voice telling you what you can't do, stand up and tell that voice to **SHUT UP!** Say to yourself, **"NO MORE STINKING THINKING!"**

The next step in making a difference is, knowing what your talents and skills are. None of us are born with an instruction manual that tells our parents what we're going to grow up to be, and sadly, not many parents pay attention to what subtle signs of excellence their children might be exhibiting. At three years old, my youngest son, Justin, showed interest in boxing.

He would take the iPad and watch videos of Xbox Kinnect boxing. He used to put socks on his hands and shadowbox against the video. When we got a Kinnect device of our own he became the undisputed champion of the house! We later gave him a pair of gloves and a spring-mounted boxing bag that he punched on every day.

He wouldn't take off his boxing gloves for the first two days after he got it! He's not ready get into a ring, but maybe in the next year or so we'll put him in karate and see how he takes to it. He may be talented, or it may be a phase. As his parents, my wife and I have to make the decision of exploring the potential for him until he can make his own decisions.

But what about those of us who are grown? What about those of you who think that you've wasted too much time? I had a woman in her 60s approach me after one of my seminars and tell me that my saying you can have, do, and become anything you want scared her. I could tell that she was genuinely disturbed because she was almost on the verge of tears.

I explained to her (like I shared with you earlier) that Col. Harland Sanders didn't succeed with his 11 herbs and spices fried chicken recipe until he was in his 70s. So ... it's never too late. As long as you have the ability to get out of your bed and face the world, you have a chance to make a difference.

Let me ask you this ... What do you do that pleases you? What do you do that makes you feel good, that you can share with others? When you can answer that question you are on your way to making a difference. I always credit Taria with being my first success story. When I helped her discover her way of making a difference by turning her hobby of taking pictures into a full-time photography business, I discovered MY passion; and ironically, my passion is helping people discover and cultivate their passions.

Let's talk about passion for a minute. How many of you can honestly say that you're passionate about your job? ... It's okay if you're not passionate about your job. What's not okay is for you to go through your life without discovering something you're passionate about. And it doesn't have to be something that makes money (although that's not necessarily a bad thing).

Some people find their passion in gardening or cooking. Some people find their passion in working out and becoming better physically fit and some have found their passion by training and coaching others to become better physically fit... And guess what? Not only are they making a difference in their own lives but also in their clients' lives. What is it that you can't stop thinking about? What is it that's the last thing on your mind before you go to sleep and the first thing on your mind when you wake up in the morning? What drives you?

It's okay if you can't answer these questions now. It's okay if you can't answer these questions tomorrow. However, it's not okay for you to not seek out the answers to these questions at all. It's not okay for you to not ever find the answers to these questions because when you find your passion, you will find your purpose, and when you find your purpose you will begin making a difference in your life and the lives of those around you.

Passion is what separates the pretenders from the contenders, and the contenders from the champions. You've got to be a pretty good athlete to be recruited by a Division I college or university, but not every good athlete makes it to the pros. Of those who make to training camp; as good as many of those athletes are, some still get cut.

As many of those athletes who do make the team, many still ride the bench while others become superstars. Passion is what separates the magnificent from the mediocre. If you want to make a difference, you're going to have to discover what your talents and skills are and become passionate about honing your talents and skills. Your passion for greatness will be what fuels your talents and skills.

Next, in being passionate about your talents and skills you have to enjoy what you're doing. If you're not enjoying yourself, why are you even bothering to do what you're doing? This is the problem 90% of people find themselves in. Thousands, if not millions of people spend 4, 6, or 8 years in college and then go out into the real world doing a job that has little or nothing to do with their field of study.

Why? Well, because bills have to be paid. Student loans have to be paid. In short, we have to survive. But let me ask you this ... Do you want to go through life LIVING or just surviving?

The Chinese philosopher, Confucius said, "Choose the work you love and you will never have to work a day in your life." Your level of passion and enjoyment is what makes the difference between having a job and having a career. Your level of passion and enjoyment is what makes the difference between having a career and following your calling.

Although I enjoyed my career in Law Enforcement, I found my passion in being a speaker, a writer and Life Coach. In fact when people would ask me what I do, I would say, "By vocation I'm a police officer, but by passion, I'm a professional speaker, writer and Life Coach."

When you love what you do it extends your life! Statistics show that cops die within 5 years of retiring. The main underlying reason is because after spending so many years on the job, when it's all over, the majority of them have nothing to transcend to. They don't have anything to do that gives them that same sense of fulfillment and purpose.

I swore I wasn't going to be one of those statistics so I began doing things that made me happy and made me money so I'd have something to move over into after my Law Enforcement career. As a speaker, writer and Life Coach, my life has a purpose that will never end.

Now I want to go back to that Confucius quote for a minute. When he said you won't have to work for the rest of your life - that is not to be taken literally.

Game time is when you get to play, but the preparation and practice required to get ready for game time is **work.** Think about how many hours are spent writing, rehearsing, producing and recording that are required for you to listen to your favorite five minute song or your favorite 15 song CD.

Think about the hundreds of shots your favorite NBA players make in practice so that they can rain 3 pointers when the game is on the line. That's **WORK.** Allen Iverson was a great ball player with a lot of pure talent but now he's broke and no team will have him. Why? **He had a poor work ethic.** If you go to YouTube and type "Allen Iverson - Practice" in the search box, you'll see videos of his ranting at a press conference about how UN-important practice was to him.

If you want to make a difference you must embrace the fact that the only place where success comes before work is in the dictionary. As Jeffrey Fox wrote in his book, "How to Become a CEO," "Glamour and glory come after grunt work."

If you want to make a difference you have to believe. You have to believe in yourself and your ability. You have to believe in your product. You have to believe in your service. If you don't believe in yourself, how can you expect others to believe in you? Why should they believe in you?

There's an African proverb that goes, "If you can conquer the enemy within, the enemy outside doesn't stand a chance." You see, again… most of the time, the first person to talk you out of your dreams and goals is not the person talking **TO** you, it's the person talking **WITHIN** you. More often than not, if you quit something, your mind was made up long before you actually quit.

You might have gone and talked to a friend, but chances are; the way you posed your situation, you made it easy for them to agree with you or encourage you to quit. When we communicate with people, we have a way of telling the story in such a way that either makes us the hero or the victim; whichever one is going to paint you in the brightest light. You have to be honest with yourself and determine if you're looking for a reason to stay in the fight or assurance in your decision to quit.

You can do amazing things when you believe in yourself. You can do the impossible when you believe in yourself. You can lose that extra weight. You can get that raise. You can get that new job. You can get that man or woman of your dreams.

How many times have you seen a dumpy looking person with a "10" on his or her arm and ask, "How did THAT happen?" Belief is the fuel you need to make the impossible possible. It was belief that proved the world wasn't flat. It was belief that put a man on the moon, and it was belief that put a black man in the Oval Office and kept him there for a second term.

If you can believe a man was beaten within an inch of his life, nailed to a cross, stabbed in the abdomen, buried in a cave; and rose from the dead three days later, how can you not believe that you can lose a few extra pounds or make a few extra dollars – especially if you have people depending on you?! Take a second and let that marinate a bit!

If you want to make a difference, you should expect to lose some friends. You see, if you want to make a difference, you yourself must BE different. You have to become something new – **someONE** new; and in a world where people find comfort in complacency, you will find that many of the people you thought had your back through thick and thin are really just fair weather friends.

They're there for you when the times are good and everything is running smooth, but if you need them to go out on a limb for you – to go out on a limb **with** you, they coincidentally have a personal crisis of their own going on at the exact same time. Do you know someone like that? If not, then you're probably that friend (smile)!

At the time of this writing, it has been ten years since I decided to become a professional speaker. I won't say that there were people who wanted to see me fail, but I will say that there were people who couldn't see me succeeding at it. You know what? In all honesty, there actually were people who wanted to see me fail. There still are and there always will be.

When I gave my first professional speech, it was a graduation keynote address ... at an 8th grade graduation ceremony at the same school I attended as a kid. When I approached Sister Patricia Hogan, the Principal – who, by the way is the same Principal I had when I was there – and asked her for the opportunity to address the class, I told her I couldn't possibly charge her. So she gave me a shot and only asked one thing of me – that I incorporate into my speech the message that with God all things are possible.

I spoke for about 25 minutes in front of about 30 graduates and their 250 some-odd relatives and friends, and I was on fire! When I was done, I got a standing ovation and Sister Patricia was in tears. Mrs. Jean Brutus, the woman who started her career as my 5th grade teacher and was now the 8th grade teacher was in tears. Before I left, the school secretary handed me a card and I went home. When I got home I opened the envelope and inside the Thank You card was $150 cash! I have since spoken there twice and have been asked to come back every year for the foreseeable future!

I called a close relative and said, "I'm a professional speaker. I just gave my first real speech!" Before I could even get to the part about the surprise in the envelope, her first response wasn't "Congratulations" or "Good Job." Her first response was, "You're not a professional until you get paid." Talk about taking the wind out of my sails! She totally ruined my mood. Needless to say, I got off the phone with her quick! Remember what I said about that Stinkin' Thinkin'. You have to have zero tolerance for Stinkin' Thinkin'. Don't accept it from yourself and don't accept it from the people around you!

You see, when you're on the path to making a difference, you have to realize that everyone that came with you this far can't go with you all the way. When your goal is to make a difference you are going to have to cut some ties, or at least distance yourself from some of the people in your life.

People are going to talk about you and most of them not to your face! They're going to say, "You done changed!" And you know what? ... They're right! You **HAVE** changed! You are making a difference in yourself and they're bearing witness to it! Making a difference is all about change and it should feel good when people notice that change happening. It feels good when you can shop at Victoria's Secret instead of Lane Bryant. It feels good when you have to take your suits to get taken in instead of being let out, and it feels good when you get that first new paycheck after getting that promotion.

If you want to make a difference you're going to have to have a larger vision of yourself and for yourself, and know that not everyone is going to share in that vision. Not everyone is going to appreciate that vision. As Les Brown says, "If they can't have a larger vision for themselves, how can they possibly have a larger vision **for YOU?!**" You are going to have to change your circle of influence.

It was Dr. Dennis Kimbro who said, "If you're the smartest person in your circle, you need a new circle." To that I would add if you're the richest person in your circle, you need a new circle. If you're the healthiest person in your circle, you need a new circle. If you want to lose weight then you can't sit with a group of people whose idea of a good time is eating unhealthy food and drinking excessively. If you're trying to quit smoking, you can't hang out with a group of smokers.

I have an older fraternity brother whom I haven't seen in years because back in the day he was heavy into drugs. He doesn't come around anymore because for him it's a trigger to a lifestyle he has been able to rid himself of. I miss him because when I was pledging he was always teaching me something, but I respect his absence and applaud his sobriety.

In the book "Think & Grow Rich," Napoleon Hill wrote about something called a "Mastermind Group." As I mentioned earlier, a mastermind group is a group of like-minded people who are united by a common goal or objective. In a mastermind group the members may be at different levels of growth, so everyone has a chance to gain a new insight towards achieving his or her individual goal. I have a tight group of about 4 or 5 friends who are also speakers. We communicate often and support each other's projects.

There's a saying that goes, "Show me who you are with and I will show you who you are." Jim Rohn said, "You are the sum of the five people you spend the most time with." Depending on what you want to do with your life, you may have to hand out some friendship pink slips. When I became a cop, there were certain social spots I could no longer go to, and if I was at a party and caught a whiff of a "particularly unique plant" being burned, I would have to leave.

There were certain people I couldn't be around. That's just the game. If you want to make a difference in your life; if you want to upgrade who you are, some of the people in your life are going to have to be downgraded. And you don't have to make a big production about letting these people go or distancing yourself. Just *fade away* to some extent.

I mean I'm not telling you to go out and hurt people's feelings or be a jerk, but if you are busy focusing on the changes you want to make, you'll find that you really don't have the time to be around those people who aren't on your same path. Your fair weather friends will come at you like, "Where you been? You act like you don't have time for us anymore." The funny thing is, they don't know how right they are and you're not "acting" like you don't have time for them, you really don't!

But like I said, you don't want to hurt anyone's feelings, so you might say something like "I'm just working on some things." Whereas your fair weather friends might take offense to your absence, your true friends will accept that response. Both might ask you what kind of "things" you are working on. This leads me right into my next point.

If you want to make a difference, you have to be very careful with whom you share your dreams, goals and activities. Remember, everyone who came with you can't go with you. You don't share your money with everyone all willy-nilly, and you should be equally if not more frugal when it comes to your dreams, goals and activities. Why? Because not everyone is going to have the same appreciation for what you envision as you do. Remember, if people can't or won't see themselves doing bigger things and they see you as their equal, how do you think they are going to see you?

As I said before, when you strive to improve yourself, you begin to violate the sanctity of the comfort zone that you occupy with your friends who are warm and cozy right where they are. These are the people who will try to talk you out of improving yourself and making a difference. These are the people who will tell you what you're not capable of, even though they may not have any experience in what you're trying to do. I call these people "Bubble Busters" and I wrote a whole chapter about them in my first book, **"FIND A WAY TO MAKE A WAY!"**

Before I began speaking, I was reading voraciously. I would read two or three books simultaneously and I would share quotes from the books I was reading on social media. I was able to determine who could stay and those from whom I had to distance myself by the way they responded to those quotes.

In order to make a difference you must be powerful. People respond to power. They are either attracted to it or they are repelled by it. In case you haven't noticed, I have a very direct style of communicating. I don't mince words and my wife has made it her life's mission to get me to be more tactful. There are people who are inspired by my words and there are some who choose to disagree, and that's okay with me.

Like I said in the beginning, take what fits for you and discard what doesn't, but whether you choose to agree or disagree with anything I'm saying, you're going to put this book down knowing that I'm coming from a place of honesty and power. Each and every one of us was born with power, but not everyone uses their power. Not everyone even knows what kind of power they possess. Not everyone believes they even have power, but we all do.

It's been said that "knowledge is power," and it's been said that "information is power." This is not entirely true. Knowledge or information that goes unapplied – that is not put to use is useless. Therefore, power comes from the use or application of knowledge and information. Imagine what kind of world we would be living in if George Washington Carver and Alexander Graham Bell did not use their *power* of invention.

Imagine what kind of world we would be living in if Martin Luther King Jr., Nelson Mandela and Mahatma Gandhi did not use their *power* to bring people to believe in equality. What will your world be like if you don't share your *power*? Zig Ziglar said, "Unless and until you do something with what you have learned, you might as well not have learned it. The person who won't read is no better off than the person who can't read."

Earlier, I spoke about discovering and honing your talents and skills. Now I am going to share with you a method that will help you go about doing so. I'm going to use the word **"P.O.W.E.R."** as an acronym, which stands for **PLAN, ORGANIZE, WONDER, ENGAGE & REPEAT.**

PLAN

Having an idea is not enough. You need a plan to achieve your goals and make that idea a reality. You need a plan to show you how you're going to achieve your goal. How long is it going to take you to achieve your goal? Set a deadline to achieve your goal. Determine what you're going to have to do. What resources are you going to need? What resources do you already have? What's going to be required of you?

How much is it going to cost you in terms of time, money and sweat equity? You need to write all of these things down. These are the elements that will make up your plan. I cannot stress enough the importance of writing these things down. An idea that you do not convert into a plan by writing it down has the same value as gas passed in the wind and smells just as bad. It was JC Penny who said, "Give me a stock clerk with a goal and I will give you a man who will make history. Give me a man with no goals and I will give you a stock clerk."

ORGANIZE

This is where you really begin to map out your plan. In the first stage you were gathering the pieces to the puzzle. Here is where you start putting those pieces together. You might not have all of the resources you need, but by organizing those that you do have you can begin mapping out how you will go about acquiring them.

The Law of Attraction states that "you attract into your life whatever you think about and focus on most. Your dominant thoughts will find a way to manifest." It is a very real and powerful thing. When you are actively working towards your goals; God, the universe, or whatever you deem your higher power to be, will provide you with the people and resources you need to help and guide you along the way.

WONDER

This is the fun part. This is the part when you get to imagine what life will be like once you've achieved your goal. Picture in your mind how good it will feel when you can go back to wearing those clothes in your closet that you couldn't fit in before. Picture in your mind how good it will feel to have your realtor hand you the keys to your dream home.

Picture in your mind what your dream home looks like. How many rooms does it have? Does it have hardwood floors or marble floors? How much land is it sitting on? Picture in your mind having enough space in which your children can play outside for hours. How does that feel?

This is called "visualization, "and it plays a powerful role in achieving your goals. Many people make what are called "Vision Boards" on which they place pictures of those things they want to achieve and attain. And if you're not the arts and crafts type, don't worry.

There's a website called Pinterest and on it you can create multiple boards from pictures you upload or find on the internet. If your goal is to lose weight and tone your body you can post pictures of people whose figure you want to see yourself having. If there's a particular car you want to drive, you can post as many pictures as your heart desires. Wondering what your future life will look like and feel like will fuel you on your journey towards making it your reality.

ENGAGE

This is the most important step. You must take action. Confucius said, "The journey of a thousand miles begins with the first step." Tony Robbins said, "Never leave the site of an idea or goal without taking a definitive action towards achieving it."

The first step towards losing weight can be that first push-up, sit-up or walk around your block. The first step towards quitting smoking can be you taking that pack of cigarettes in your pocket or purse and throwing it in the garbage without taking that one last smoke. I knew I had to get myself back in the gym, so I went to work out with another one of my fraternity brothers who's a competitive body builder. He kicked my butt, but he also kick started me into going back to the gym regularly, and along with good eating and cutting beer totally out of my diet, I stand here today 25 pounds lighter!

Again let me remind you, eleven years ago (2005) I made a conscious decision to put down my PlayStation and pick up books. My mindset was that I wanted to read books that would get my mind right so that I could get my money right. The first action I took was to pick up a book called "Rich Dad/Poor Dad" by Robert Kiyosaki.

Reading that book is what gave me the tools I shared with my wife to get her to start her business, and what lead me to becoming a motivational speaker. I figured if I could get **this woman** to actually listen to me and produce results, I can speak to and motivate anyone!

You have to take action in order to produce results. If you want to produce results in your life you are going to have to avoid the people in the **"Gonna' But"** family. These are the people who always say, "I was gonna do that, but ..." or "I'm gonna do that, but ..."

How many of you know people in the **"Gonna' But"** family? How many of you are members of the **"Gonna' But"** family? Well after today I want you to divorce yourself from that family because nothing comes after "but" except a bunch of stinkin' thinkin', and if you don't take action, you will never be able to make a difference. So while taking some form of action is important; the next step is equally as important, and that step is to ...

REPEAT

The next time you're at the supermarket, pick up a bottle of hair conditioner. Depending on the brand, you may find directions on the bottle that say "rinse and repeat?" Let me tell you, that life works in the exact same way. In order to insure you're getting the job done, you have to repeat your actions.

Say to yourself, **"Success begets success."** Now let me ask you this, do you have a job in which you only show up for one day? Of course not. You go back to work every day because you have to repeat what you do in order to get paid. If you want to make a difference in your life and in the lives of others, you will have to repeat what you do.

Martin Luther King Jr. didn't give just one speech or go on one march. Mother Theresa didn't just feed one group of people, she fed and cared for thousands. When I read "Rich Dad/Poor Dad," I didn't just stop at that book. The foundation and success of my career comes from reading book after book after book, and now I write them too!

Who goes to the gym and only does one push up, one sit up, or one rep on the weights? If you only did one rep, why bother going to the gym at all. It would be a waste of time, right? Whatever you want to succeed at doing you are going to have to develop a habit of repetition. One of my high school teachers used to always say, "Repetition is the mother of all skill."

When you started doing your job, you had to be taught how to do it, but after a while you were doing it on your own and now the job is second nature to you. The same principle applies to every other facet in your life. If you want to make a difference you will have to use this formula in its entirety.

So let's review:

PLAN: Map out what it is you want to do and what will be required of you to do it. Remember ... never leave the site of a goal without taking some kind of definitive action towards achieving it ... and **WRITING IT DOWN** could be that first step!

ORGANIZE: Pull your resources together.

WONDER: Imagine what your life will be like after you've achieved your objective.

ENGAGE: Take action. **Do SOMETHING.**

REPEAT: Repetition is the mother of all skill. Keep doing what you're doing so you can become proficient and then keep doing it over and over again still so that you can become excellent at it.

Now ... Let's talk about what happens once you've become good at what you do, because this can be a very dangerous part of your journey. You see, once you become good at something, once it becomes easy to do you run the risk of getting comfortable. When people get comfortable they become complacent, and when people become complacent, they run the risk of regressing.

When things get too easy to do, that's when you start taking shortcuts to make things even easier. You start making exceptions to the rule, and eventually the exceptions become the rule and if you've created a habit of taking shortcuts you may lose sight of the skills that made you at one time excellent. Be honest, how many of you are guilty of this? ... I won't tell anybody – I promise!

I am sure you either know, are, or have been that person who got into a nice groove on your/their job and your/their attitude was, "I'm good right where I am ... Leave me alone to do my thing ... If I don't bother anybody nobody will bother me." That's cool if you want to just let the world pass you by, but if you are going to make a difference, you have to seek out challenges in order to sharpen your skills.

When I was in third grade my Principal, Mr. Rathjens, called my mother into his office and advised her to take me out of the public school system because, in his words, staying there would have done me a disservice in the long run. He told my mother that I was a pain in the butt to my teachers, not because I was a bad kid, but because I would finish my work early and start helping my friends with their work, which annoyed the teachers ... especially since I was showing them shortcuts that worked (shortcuts that she taught me by the way)!

So my mother put me in Catholic school. Remember that principal I was telling you about, Sister Patricia? Let me tell you ... That woman did not play! She has been a principal for over fifty years and she hasn't missed a beat! She didn't take any foolishness from me, or any other kid. She challenges every kid to be more than just another inner city kid. She challenges every kid to believe that they can and **will** go to college and make something out of themselves.

Let me tell you ... By the time I was in the eighth grade, I had had enough of Catholic school! When we had to take our end of the year tests and write down the schools where we wanted our scores to go, I wrote down the names of the two public high schools in my city – and I just **KNEW** my days of wearing a tie to school were over ... All the way up until Sister Patricia had the same talk with my father that Mr. Rathjens had with my mother. And she herself submitted my test scores to Essex Catholic Boys High School, the only Catholic high school in my city.

However, I thank God for both Mr. Rathjens and Sister Patricia because without them putting me in those challenging environments, I could have easily wound up like some of the guys I grew up with ... Guys I wound up locking up when I became a cop, or seeing do the "junkie-lean" because they were hooked on drugs.

You see, you **must** challenge yourself in order to grow and improve. People who are complacent will tell you, "I'm happy right where I am." **I'm telling you now to run from these people like your life depends on it because it does!** These people are toxic and they will infect you with a case of chronic laziness that will kill you years before they actually put you in the ground! **Always Be Challenging yourself!"** and put them on your bedroom and bathroom mirrors as well as on your refrigerator and desk at work so you see them all day every day.

Complacent people will say, "I could've done that, but I didn't want to mess up what I have." These people are full of it! People aren't afraid of failure ... They're afraid of succeeding! Why? Because in order to succeed, you have to work hard, and once you've reached one level of success you have to work at that same level to maintain it – and work even harder to reach the next level of success. The "Could've Buts" are the cousins of the "Gonna Buts."

Early in my law enforcement career, one of my training officers told me the reason why he never took a promotion exam was because the only gun he wanted to be responsible for was the one on his hip. Yet another one of my co-workers went from Patrolman to Captain in about 10 years because right after he took one promotion exam, he began studying for the next one. He challenged himself constantly and he was only about one-third of the way through his career.

However, not everyone is such a self-starter. That's why it's best to have a mentor, trainer or coach. That's why I have coaches and mentors and that's why I belong to a Mastermind Group. My friends in that group challenge me and hold me accountable. That's why I received my certification as a Life Coach. I challenge my clients to see where they are now and envision how they can go about improving their lives, their relationships and their businesses, and I hold them accountable to the goals they set for themselves.

Whether they want to admit it or not, everyone is motivated by the approval of others to some degree, but the person whose approval must be most important to you is your own. **You know** when you're giving it your all, and **you know** when you're slacking. One thing I learned from my military and police academy training instructors is that just when you think you don't have anything left, if you push a little bit harder, you'll find that last bit of fight you need to get you across the goal line. I had them to push me. I have my mastermind friends to push me. And you **ME** to push you!

Speaking about challenging yourself, do you remember the Gatorade commercial with basketball players Kevin Durant and Dwayne Wade? Kevin Durant wakes up in a cold sweat because he dreamt he was going for a dunk which got rejected by Dwayne Wade, and you see him training hard while consuming Gatorade products. The next thing you know he's slamming the ball in Wade's face and Wade wakes up in a cold sweat and starts training.

Once while attending a seminar with the U.S. Marshals I remember seeing a poster that had a picture of a guy lifting weights wearing a t-shirt that said "PRISONER," and the underlying caption said, "Every day you're not working out, **HE IS.**" In order to make a difference, you must, must, must challenge yourself!

The last thing I want to share with you about making a difference is this ... If you want to make a difference you must have a will to win. In order to have this will to win you must not beat yourself up over your past mistakes, and you must not allow the fears of your past or present to keep you from winning. Fear is also an acronym, which stands for "False Evidence Appearing Real." More often than not, what you're afraid of and what you have to face are two very different things.

I remember my first night at boot camp. I was 19 years old and I was the farthest I had ever been from home. Because I didn't consult my family about my decision to enlist, I have always credited my enlisting in the Air Force as my first decision as a man. I made a decision about my life that they had no say in and I had put myself in a position where they could not rescue me. No matter what; like it or not, I was committed to the United States Air Force. I signed a contract and I took an oath.

So there I was … let off the bus in front of the dormitory I'd spend the next six weeks in with about sixty dudes who I didn't know from the crickets chirping in the Texas night. By the way, no matter where you come from or what time of day you left there, everyone arrives at Lackland Air Force Base; San Antonio, Texas during the hours of night.

So there we all were … Standing at the position of attention just as the airmen on the bus ride taught us. No one said a word because they told us to be quiet and not speak until spoken to. It was 70 degrees **at night**, but I swear to you that you could hear teeth chattering and knees shaking and my knees were shaking too, but then I told myself to calm down.

In my mind I was literally cracking jokes to myself - and this is what I said, word for word … "What are you scared of? Ain't nothin' you can do about it now. Wouldn't it be funny if two big barrel-chested country boys just came out here spittin' tobacco and cussin' like in the movies?" And just a few seconds later … **"JESUS H. CHRIST!! WHAT IN THE ***** DO WE HAVE HERE?!"**

Their names were Sgt. Ed Muncy and Sgt. Franklin Skidmore. They came out just as I had imagined it, and let me tell you that I never heard so many insults spit out at one time. And to be completely honest with you ... I was too busy fighting to keep from busting out laughing to be scared, and by the time Sgt. Skidmore got to me, the "Jersey" in me came out. Not cocky, but confident, and as shaken as I was on the inside, this dude wasn't going to see it. By the time we were through with our exchange, I was placed in charge of the 30 of those men who made up my Basic Training class.

The lesson I learned that night will be the lesson I will share with you now. I call it "The 3 F's," which stand for *"Face it, Fight it & Free yourself from it."* When you face your fear; whatever it is, you see it exactly for what it is. Don't kid yourself and don't feed into it even more. Next you have to fight it. You have to take some form of action that goes directly against whatever it is you're afraid of. How do you fight your fear?

Use your **P.O.W.E.R.** ... **Plan** your attack; **Organize** your resources; **Wonder** what life will be like when you've conquered your fear; **Engage** your plan of attack; and until you have conquered your fear... **REPEAT!** You face your fear ... You fight that fear, and you keep fighting and fighting and fighting until finally you conquer that fear, and once you've conquered your fear, you will be free from it!

In closing, let us review what we've discussed. If you want to make a difference – be it in your life or the lives of others, you have to:

1. Beware and rid yourself of any stinkin' thinkin'. Do not allow it to talk you out of your destiny!

2. Know your talents and skills!

3. Be passionate and enjoy what you're doing!

4. Be willing to put in the necessary work!

5. Believe in yourself. Believe in your ability!

6. Expect to lose some old friends and gain some new ones!

7. Have a larger vision for yourself!

8. Be careful who you share your dreams and goals with!

9. Discover and use your **P.O.W.E.R. ... PLAN, ORGANIZE, WONDER, ENGAGE, and REPEAT!**

10. **"A.B.C." ... Always Be Challenging yourself!**

11. Have a will to win. Overcome your fear ... Remember **"The 3F's" ... Face it, Fight it & Free yourself from it!**

If you don't remember anything else, I want you to remember that winners have reasons and losers have excuses. A reason is just cause for taking a different path to achieve your objective. An excuse is a crappy justification for why you quit. A reason will allow people to keep believing in you even when you switch lanes, but an excuse is more for you to talk **yourself** into believing why you failed to act or press on.

You see, there's nothing wrong with changing your mind about something or realizing you've hit a dead end. But what do you do when you're traveling someplace, realize you've made a wrong turn and hit a dead end? Do you just unpack your car and look for a place to live on that dead end street? You'd be surprised how many people actually do that with their lives. They hit a hard patch and they stop. They quit. They give up on themselves. Don't let this be you. In life it doesn't matter how many times you get knocked down as long as you get up one time more than you get knocked down.

If you can change the life of just one person; even if that first person is yourself, you will find yourself on the path towards success.

Chapter Seven
Don't Say "NO" to Yourself Any Longer!

People do not become failures because others have told them "no." People become failures because they say "no" to themselves! As human beings, we all come from the same genetic stuff. We come into this world as blank slates and empty sponges. Wherever God saw fit to drop us off on this planet, we have to make due with whatever resources we have available to us.

Therefore, I submit to you that if you take an infant of any given ethnicity or nationality, and raise him or her in a culture completely opposite of that infant's original nationality, that infant's personality will grow and develop based upon that culture wherein which it was raised. So ultimately, you get what you got and you rock with it!

There is no sense in wishing you were born somewhere else or wishing that you were born someone else. You are who you are, where you are; and if you're not happy with who you are and or where you are, then it's up to you to change who you are and where you are!

Once again, I can practically read your mind right now. You are likely thinking "that's easier said than done!" Or "why don't you just tell me how to do it then?!" Well first off, you don't get off that easily. Changing who you are or what your condition is, is not an easy thing to do - nor is it supposed to be. If it were easy to go from "ain't got" to "got plenty," everyone would be doing it and there would be virtually no poverty in the world.

But there are only a select few who actually realize this and put it to work in their lives. As for the other side of the coin ... those who are thinking "Why don't you just tell me how to do it then?!" I cannot tell each and every individual what he or she needs to do in each of their lives. But you see, these are the people who are looking for someone to blame when beset with the setbacks that come along the way of bettering oneself.

You want me to tell you exactly where you invest your money. You want me to tell you each and every move I made on my journey. Well that's not going to happen. It's like the old proverb "give a man a fish, he eats for a day. Teach him how to fish, and you'll eat for the rest of his life." I must admit, when I first began my journey of improving myself, I too wanted the answers spoon-fed to me. But the more I read; the more and more I studied, the more I realized that I wasn't being given fish - I was being taught how to fish, and "fishing" is nothing more than implementing into your life that which you have learned.

So it all comes down to you! Yeah, it would be nice if someone came along and just gave you a million dollars, but since that's not likely to happen should you want that million dollars any less? Of course not ... that just doesn't make any sense. If you want that million dollars, what's stopping you from getting it yourself? ... YOU. You see, when it comes down to it, it is never the voices talking to you that talk you out of reaching for and achieving your goals and turning your dreams into your reality. It is *always* the voice *within you* that does that.

Sometimes my wife, Taria, and I often joke with one another when asking for something to get done. One of us will say, "You can't tell me what to do. You don't own me!" Her favorite is, "You're not the boss of me – you don't own my soul!" Again, these are jokes between she and I, but what I want you to do is begin to seriously internalize these statements. The next time someone tells you that you should give up and quit, you need to say – even if only to yourself, *"You can't tell me what to do!"*

Even in the workplace, where more and more, people think, believe, and act as if their title and position is a representation or validation of who they are – and some have no problem letting you know, you must be able to say to yourself, *"You're not the boss of ME – you don't own my soul!"* You see, they may be the boss of your *position*, but they are not the boss of *YOU!* You must be bold enough to say – even if only to yourself (in the words of the poet William Ernest Henley), *"I am the master of my fate. I am the captain of my soul."*

There is only but one person on the face of this planet capable of killing your dreams. There is only but one person on the face of this planet capable of holding you back and holding you down. It's not your mother, father, brother, sister, cousin, friend, fiancée, husband, wife, son, daughter, uncle, aunt, boss, subordinate, or any stranger walking the street or prancing across your television screen.

That one person is the person you see in the mirror. That one person is the person who knows what you're going to say before you open your mouth. That person is the person who knows where you're going to go and what you're going to do before you take a single step. That person is **YOU.** Do not allow yourself to deprive you of all the greatness you deserve. Don't say "NO" to yourself any longer!

Chapter Eight
The Value of Ignorance

One thing that really amazes me is how people function on what they *think* they know more so than what they actually know. A lot of times; dare I say more than 90% of the time we learn new words by hearing them around us. We'll hear a new word on television, on the radio, overhearing someone else's conversation; or in direct conversation, and we may not know the literal definition of the word, but we get a feel for the word based on the context of the conversation.

If the word resonates with us, we will add it into our vocabulary and we will go on using it, and often without ever looking up the word. Now, a good portion of the time people get away with this, but then there are those occasional times when a person throws a word out there that they have absolutely no business using. This is a prime example of ignorance.

As a matter of fact, the word "ignorance" in and of itself is an even better example of what I am saying. One sure-fire way to insult someone is to call him or her "ignorant." However, if the context in which the word is being used is factual; it's not an insult, it's simply a factual observation. Contrary to popular belief, "ignorance" does not mean an absence of intelligence. It means a lack of knowledge. The difference may be subtle, but then to better solidify the difference we'll have to examine the difference between intelligence and knowledge.

According to the Merriam-Webster Dictionary, intelligence means, "the ability to learn or understand or to deal with new or trying situations; *ALSO,* the skilled use of reason." The word knowledge means "the fact or condition of knowing something with familiarity gained through experience or association." Therefore to be ignorant simply means not knowing *about something ... NOT* not knowing *anything.*

The fact of the matter is that there are a great many things about which people are ignorant, but because they misunderstand the true meaning of the word, you will not likely come across someone who is readily willing to acknowledge their ignorance. However, this is yet another reason why so many people fail to reach new levels of success. If you do not admit or acknowledge that a problem exists, or your lack of knowledge, how can you go about solving or correcting it?

Something I always say is that when people make mistakes and suffer self-caused setbacks, it's basically because either they made a mistake of ignorance or they made a mistake of arrogance. When you make a mistake of ignorance, you simply didn't know any better. However, a mistake of arrogance occurs when you actually do know better than to follow a particular course of action, but act anyway. This is the cause of most people's failures in life. Just ask any convict who has accepted accountability for his or her present condition behind bars.

There is a Chinese proverb that says, **"When the student is ready, the teacher will appear."** The value of ignorance is in seeing it for what it is ... a lack of knowledge. Once you find yourself lacking in knowledge, you can go about filling that void and improving your life. There is absolutely nothing wrong with acknowledging your ignorance. In fact, the acknowledgement of one's ignorance is the dawn of one's intelligence. There is absolutely nothing wrong with saying "I don't know." It's better to say "I don't know" than it is to fabricate an explanation and embarrass yourself. As the saying goes, "It is better to remain silent and be thought a fool than to open your mouth and remove all doubt."

In his song, "True To Myself," the R&B singer Eric Benet sings, "A lie could be the gospel truth if eloquently told." If someone comes to you with a question to which you don't know the answer, you are insulting their faith in you as an intelligent person by giving them an answer you're creating on the fly. God forbid they believe you and repeat the nonsense you told them to someone who knows better. You just made your friend look like a fool and how do you think you now look to him or her?

Now, you might have some knowledge in what you're saying, but not necessarily know all the facts. Hey ... That's okay! All you have to do is speak to what you do know and acknowledge that which you don't. The other option is speak to *only* that which you know. There's nothing wrong with saying "If memory serves correctly," then speak to what you believe, but you've acknowledged that you might be mistaken.

The other option is saying, "I'm not certain so I'd rather not say." Here, you're also acknowledging that there's something you don't know, so instead of possibly committing yourself to an error, you'd rather say nothing at all. You can't be wrong about what you don't say!

From now on, ask yourself, "What *don't* I know about...?" This is the key that opens the door to gaining knowledge because success doesn't come from having all the right answers, it comes from being able to ask all the right questions. Asking the right questions and then seeking out the answers for yourself gives you the ability to have the answers available for the people who come up behind you with questions.

Most people don't realize this until the people coming up to them with questions happen to be their children. However, remember, there's nothing wrong with saying "I don't know," so if this happens with your child, turn the situation into a learning moment in which you go about showing your child how to seek out the answer. It might mean going onto Google, or actually taking a trip to the library or to the museum.

In the end, there is nothing wrong with being ignorant as long as you are willing to learn from your ignorance. Again, ignorance is the lack of knowledge – not the absence of intelligence. It takes intelligence to be able to know that you don't know so that you can learn to know what you don't know. Once you know what you didn't know, you've begun to grow, and when you know you know what you know, no one can take it away from you.

There is value in ignorance. That value is found in knowing that ignorance is nothing more than an empty cup in your mind yearning to be filled. It is like an empty stomach yearning to be fed. If you do not feed your body, in time it will cease to function. If you do not feed it well, it will function poorly before ceasing to function at all. The value of ignorance is hunger.

It is a hunger for knowledge. It is a hunger that you must feed in order to quell. Just as you must always feed your body, you must always feed your mind. Your stomach rumbles to let you know you your body is hungry. Unfortunately, there's no such rumbling sensation for your mind, so you must constantly feed it.

Chapter Nine
The Value of Hard Work & Networking
(An Entrepreneur's Perspective)

An entrepreneur was so frustrated with his search for money that he went into a church to pray to God for help. While he was kneeling in the pew, he heard a deep voice from above say *"DO NOT GIVE UP HOPE."* The entrepreneur said, "Is that you God?" *"Yes,"* came the reply *"It is I, the Lord."* The entrepreneur said, "Lord, I've been trying to raise a million dollars for what seems like a million years."

The Lord said, *"Remember, a million years to you is like a second to me."* "What's a million dollars like, Lord?" asked the entrepreneur. *"A million dollars is like a penny to me,"* He responded. "Then can I have one of your pennies, Lord?" the entrepreneur asked. *"Yes,"* said the Lord ... *"In a second!"*

If you're an entrepreneur and you can relate to that kind of frustration, say *"YES LORD!"* I want you to understand something. Everyone is an entrepreneur. We all have a product to sell and a service to provide. *You* are your product, and whatever you do with your life is the service you provide. However, when you sell your product and provide your services to the benefit of others more so than yourself, you then become an employee.

When we spend our lives applying for jobs, we are marketing and promoting ourselves. When we get those jobs, we're selling ourselves, and being compensated in the form of our paychecks. The only problem is we're not the ones who make the determination of how much those paychecks are going to be. However, what separates us from millions of others; we came to the realization that we can provide a service to this world and benefit ourselves in the process.

I read a long a time ago that 90% of the world's wealth is owned by 10% of the world's population. Now, I don't know if those numbers are exact today, or if they were even exact back then, but I can appreciate the principle. I can appreciate the fact that there are more people **watching** TV than there are people **on** TV. When my wife and I went to see Prince in concert a few years back, the arena was practically sold out, but aside from Prince, there were no more than 10 or 11 people on the stage. Although there are always more people in the audience than there are on the television or on the stage, it's those people we see on television and on that stage that are walking away with all the money!

Ultimately, successful people will always be in the minority because successful people **do more.** Joe Jackson put all nine of his kids on stage yet, only Michael and Janet rose to the top. The rap label "Rocafella Records" was started by three friends; Damon Dash, Kareem Burke, and Shawn "Jay-Z" Carter, but of those three, today, Jay Z is the only one that's a household name.

How? Why? ... **He did more.** Michael Jordan was cut from his high school's varsity basketball team, yet he became the best to ever play the game. How? Why? ... **He did more.** They put more out there. None of these people whom I've named achieved their success alone, but they rose to the top because they **did more** than the people next to them.

Once upon a time three mice fell into a bucket of cream. They all started kicking to stay afloat, but after about a minute, one mouse gave up and drowned, another minute or two later, the second mouse gave up and drowned, but the third mouse kept kicking so hard that he churned that cream into butter and climbed out of that bucket! The fact of the matter is, not everyone is going to work as hard as you. With that, I want to now speak to you about the importance of networking.

True entrepreneurs are the ones who have either already shed the shackles of slave-employment or are striving to be free of those shackles. We are the ones who will not have to worry about how our children's college educations will be paid for, or how the mortgage or car note is going to be paid. We're here because we are willing to **do more!**

Maybe you're looking for the right vehicle to take you where you want to go. Maybe you're providing people with that vehicle. Either way, we are all destined to **have more** in the future because we are willing to **do more** right now! I cannot guarantee you how long it will take, but I can guarantee you that if you have a viable product or service to offer, there is a person out there willing to pay for it. The challenge is making the right connection between those looking for the right product or service and those providing them.

Sure, we can all do it on our own, but it's going to be incredibly difficult. Imagine how easier and better the outcome would have been for those mice in the parable above if they all had worked together to survive. But that wasn't meant to be.

Why do it on our own when we don't have to? Why not create a team or a series of networks to facilitate our needs ... not only our needs, but the needs of everyone that comes within our circle of influence as well? George C. Fraser, creator of FraserNet, the number one network for black professionals worldwide wrote a book called "Success Runs in Our Race," in which he refers to networking as the new "underground railroad" to freedom in the 21st century.

Is networking hard? Well that depends on what your definition of hard is. I used to work with a guy who could and would strike up a conversation with anyone; especially pretty women! This guy really had the gift of gab. Now I was a bit more reserved in my demeanor back then, so that particular trait of his rather annoyed me. However, as I began to redevelop myself and decided that I wanted to become a speaker, I had to find and develop that very trait.

What's funny is my wife calls me a "social butterfly" because whenever we go places, I almost always come across at least one person I know. We went to a comedy show at Caroline's Comedy Club in New York City and two of the comedians there came and sat with us after their sets.

One I knew because she did a lot of shows in my local area, and the other was Bill Bellamy. It just so happened that I was in grade school with his sister and I used to see a lot of his shows before he became famous. I told you we went to see Prince last year. I came across several old friends that evening - including the woman I broke up with in order to be with my wife!

Here's the thing ... Many people think that networking is all about making new contacts and forging new partnerships and connections. This is partly true ... but what about the friendships, partnerships and connections you already have? Thanks to Facebook, I've been reunited with more old friends than meeting new ones - and my old friends are in a variety of fields. The reason why I am able to connect with so many people ... even those whom I haven't seen in years is that I don't burn bridges.

I want you try an experiment ... Dig out your high school year book and do a Facebook or Google search on everyone in your class. Remember, this is the Information Age, so chances are if your classmates are out there making things happen in the world you can find them through Facebook and or Google. Imagine my surprise when I discovered that one of my high school classmates produces television shows on both the BET and TV-One networks!

What better way to build a networking base that to get reacquainted with people you already know? Again, it's not about getting something for yourself. As you reacquaint yourself with these people, work on rebuilding the friendship you once had - and even if you didn't really get along as teenagers, who's to say you might not be able to do so as adults?

Rebuild your friendship knowing that there might be someone you can send to them and perhaps someone they can send to you. ***This is networking!*** Think about each of your personal individual networks. Each of you knows at least 20 people who need a variety of products and services - many of which can be provided by people the people in your network or the next person's network.

We are all connected. Think of all the people you know and then imagine being able to help any one of them by connecting them with someone in the network you have been able to create. Think of each and every one of you doing that very same thing over and over again. ***We are all connected.***

Chapter Ten
5 Reasons Why You Are Not Succeeding

Well... we're just about at the end of our journey together, so I'm going to dive right into this chapter with no preamble. In a nutshell, I can give you five reasons why you're not succeeding...

1. <u>You Don't Believe You Can & Don't Even Believe You're Meant To.</u>

If people did not believe in themselves, we'd still be living in the wilderness. There's something about the human spirit that, when once tapped into, people become unstoppable. The human spirit is like an ocean. You can sail across it, surf along it; and or dive deep into it and swim. Or, like most people you can be afraid of it and stay out of it entirely. The people who stay out of the ocean of their potential; those who refuse to tap into their human spirit, sadly these are the masses of mediocrity.

There is so much that you are capable of that you're not even tapping into, and if you allow where you were born, where you grew up, how much or little education you have or how much money you *don't* have to keep you from tapping into your human spirit, you haven't lost the game... You never even entered the game.

If you get on the field and get bumped and bruised, that's fine. If you don't initially achieve your goal, that's fine too. But to never even enter the game? To stay sitting on your couch flipping channels watching a whole bunch of other people live out their dreams and wonder why nothing good ever comes your way? That is the definition of a loser mentality.

And if you do not check it, you will become a self-fulfilling prophecy for failure.

2. <u>You Have a Low "Accountability to Blame" Ratio.</u>

Sometimes, no matter hard you've worked or how well you've planned and prepared, things don't turn out the way you wanted them to. Take your favorite sport – take any sport... You've got two teams or two players, both stepping onto the field of battle with the hopes to come out victorious, but when the final buzzer buzzes or the last point is scored, only one of them goes home with the win.

Somewhere along the line something didn't go according to plan. Perhaps as prepared as you were, the other competitor was more prepared, or there were circumstances that you may have overlooked. That's okay... Really, it's okay. Those competitors don't just fold up and go home. They go back to the locker room and review their moves. What happens after most games – and especially in boxing and MMA? The losing players and coaches stand before the media and take accountability for their performance. I'm telling you that you have to do the same.

Unfortunately, most people in life don't do this. Remember... it's always someone else's fault why they didn't get that promotion or why they were late turning in a project or assignment. The "accountability to blame" ratio is a means of examining the outcome of your situation.

How much of what happened was your fault (accountability) or something/someone else's (blame)? Now sometimes the cards are stacked against you. People will plot and scheme and cheat to beat you... Okay, but you still have to account for yourself. Regardless of why you lost, what I am telling you is that you have to be brutally honest with yourself and count your flaws.

If you did everything you possibly could have done and still lost out, then look at what your opposition did or look at the circumstances that unfolded against you. Look to learn what went wrong so you can incorporate those things into your game plan for the next time you go to tackle that obstacle. That way you turn the loss into a lesson, and as long as you learned one or more new ways to improve yourself, you haven't really lost.

If every time there are more factors of blame than there are for accountability when you examine your "accountability to blame" ratio, you're either the most unluckiest person in the world or you're not being honest with yourself, and I doubt you're *that* unlucky.

3. <u>You Don't Have the Right People Around You.</u>

There's a saying that goes, "Show me who you're with and I will show you who you are." There's another saying that goes, "If you're around four broke people, you are guaranteed to be the fifth." In many of his speeches and books, Zig Ziglar has said that you are the average sum of the five people you spend most of your time with, and yet there's another saying that goes "You can't soar like an eagle if you're pecking around with the pigeons."

What kind of people are in your circle? Do they motivate you to be better than you are or do they encourage you to be less than you are? There's such a thing called your "sphere of influence." A sphere is nothing but a circle. Who is inside your circle and what value do they bring to you? Chances are, if you're not where you want to be in your life, those closest to you are not where want to be either.

So now the questions you must ask yourself are:

- Do they want more for themselves?
- Do I want more for myself?

If the answer to either of those questions is no, then you've got some serious soul searching to do because if the people closest to you don't want more for themselves, but you do, then you're going to have to either cut some ties or minimize the time you spend with them so you can reallocate that time to improving yourself and just occasionally hang out with them for recreation. And if you don't want more for yourself, well... There's nothing more to be said. Just pack it in and let life happen to you. No, that's not very motivational, but if you don't to get up and make a difference in your life, then I don't want to waste any more of your time, *and I certainly won't allow you to waste mine.*

I'm not saying burn bridges and cut off relationships that may have been years in the making, but going back to the "ocean" metaphor, if you're in the middle of the ocean, do you want to be with people who have given up and are allowing themselves to drown or are you going to fight to keep up with and be one of the survivors?

You should always be striving to meet and surround yourself with people who will challenge, empower and encourage you to grow and be better than you are. We live in the era of social networking and social media. Millions of people are swimming around aimlessly in the ocean of social media and millions of people are swimming around in the ocean of social networking, but those who are successful are using social media as a means of social networking. Personally speaking I have used both to meet fellow speakers, celebrities, millionaires and even the woman with whom I married.

Dr. Dennis Kimbro has said, "If you're the smartest person in your circle, then you need a new circle." To that I would add if you're the smartest, most resourceful or most successful person in your circle; if you're at the top of the food chain in any way in your circle, then you need a new circle. I'm not saying you have to always or ever be the least of anything amongst those with whom you associate, but you definitely want to have people around you that you can look up to and learn from.

If you truly want to move up from failure and mediocrity to success, evaluate, reevaluate, and re-reevaluate your relationships and make the necessary changes. It might be painful in some instances, but it will definitely be worth it. You must realize the fact that not everyone that has come with you this far can go with you the rest of the way.

4. <u>You Are Not Reading and Consuming Quality Information.</u>

Do you read? Don't feel too bad if you don't – not many people do. As a matter of fact, no – change that... DO feel bad about it. Feel really bad about it. Feeling bad about it might be the catalyst you need to change that bad habit. Most people don't read after they finish school except for newspapers, entertainment and gossip magazines, and with all of the blogs out there now fewer people are even reading those. The print publishing industry is taking a beating to the ease of online information. What kind of television do you watch? Does your television consumption consist solely of talk shows, reality shows, game shows and sports? How are those shows improving your life?

How do you think your body will respond if you do not exercise and all you feed it is fast food, candy, soda and alcohol? In time, your body is going to reflect your mistreatment of it. Your body will gradually begin to fail you. Your mind is no different. If all you feed your mind is trash print, Love & Hip Hop, Red Neck Island, Jersey Shore (yes that show is still running repeats in syndication) and other kinds of pointless content, how do you think your mind will process that content and manifest itself in what you say and do?

One of the things I have always prided myself on is my ability to have an intelligent conversation with people far more educated and professional than I. Many times people asked me what school I went to, and I was cool with being able to slide by saying "I went to Rutgers." They naturally assumed that I "graduated" from Rutgers University and kept it moving. If asked when I graduated, I'd honestly tell them that I did not graduate, but by that time we've already established such a good rapport that it didn't matter, but over time it began to matter *to me,* and I made the decision to go back to school and finish college.

I didn't do it for a job (I had been retired for two years when I went back to school). I did it for me. In my last semester of college, I watched a movie called "The Patriot" with Mel Gibson. I also watched "Glory" with Denzel Washington. I had seen these movies before, but because I was also taking a history class emphasizing on American wars, both of these movies took on a whole new meaning because I had been reading about the Revolutionary and Civil Wars.

I was always a reader though. I've been a recreational reader my whole life. I came from a family of teachers. Both of my grandmothers were teachers and I have an aunt who was an academic, the first "Dr." in my family. I have another aunt who was like my private library. When I was a teen, she asked me about a particular TV show I was watching and she hipped me to a series a books upon which the show was based. *And the books were far better than the show!*

However, I reached a point in my late 20's when I wanted to better myself (without having to go back to school), so I began reading non-fiction books – self-help/motivational books. Little did I know then that I was the planting seeds that would blossom into me finding my own life's passion, which is helping and motivating people.

I'm not saying you have to read motivational books (other than this one) or follow a bunch of motivational speakers (other than me), but what I am saying is that if you want to improve your life you have to feed your mind content that will stretch your imagination as well as strengthen and broaden your intellect. There will always be more people reading those entertainment magazines and on those reality shows than those in and on them, but the people in those entertainment magazines and reality shows are the ones getting paid.

Of all the books I have read, I can tell you which ones directly influenced me to have better work and interpersonal relationships. One book in particular, "Rich Dad Poor Dad" by Robert Kiyosaki, gave me the mental tools to:

- Move out of a 2 bedroom apartment into a 4 bedroom house
- Motivate my wife to start her own photography business
- Start my own business as a speaker, writer and Life Coach

What could you read or watch that could give you an upper hand in life? The most successful people in the world (outside of but perhaps including some entertainers and athletes) have one thing in common. They have libraries in their home. I don't necessarily mean they have a room in their homes with wall to wall books, but they definitely have two or more book cases with shelves filled end to end with books.

Do yourself a favor and start by dedicating just an hour a week reading something other than the newspaper or an entertainment magazine. Set aside a couple hours on Sunday to watch a documentary on Netflix. In time you'll find yourself spending more time reading and watching constructive content and in more time you'll find yourself feeling more knowledgeable... because you will be. Who knows, like me, you just might come across that one book that changes your life drastically for the better.

5. <u>You Spend More Time Making Excuses Than Taking Action.</u>

Believe it or not, this is the number one reason why most people don't go far in life. A whole lot of people want more for themselves, but their excuses to do nothing far exceed their reasons for doing anything. People either have a laundry list of people and circumstances to blame for them not being where they want to be in life when all they are doing is ignoring and neglecting the one person solely responsible for their current and future circumstances... *themselves.*

What are your goals? That's a very specific question. I'm not asking you what your desires or dreams are. I'm asking you what your goals are. Your dreams and desires are the embryo, but your goals are the baby, and your results are the beings your babies grow into. You see, when you have a goal you have a defined destination, an objective to be reached and achieved, but there is only one thing that separates goals from dreams and desires… ***ACTION.*** If you know what it is you want in life, but you're not taking any action towards achieving it – but you keep talking about it, then you're procrastinating, and I always say that procrastination is like masturbation… ***In the end you're only screwing yourself.***

Remember what JC Penney said, "Show me a stock clerk with a plan and I will show you a man who can make history. Show me a man without a plan and I will show you a stock clerk." Anthony Robbins teaches that once you've created a goal you must not walk away from it without taking some form of action towards achieving it. Zig Ziglar used to say that people without goals are like ships sailing aimlessly without a rudder, subject to wherever the waves of chance takes them.

One of my cardinal rules is that you can have and be anything you want in this life, provided you are willing to put in the work necessary to achieve it. The world only owes you 2 things: a place to live & a place to die. Everything in between is up to you. You can make all the excuses as to why you're not where you want to be in life, but if you haven't taken one step towards improving yourself, you know what you're full of and you know it doesn't smell pretty. In time, that stink becomes obvious to everyone… ***They just might not tell you or talk about it to your face.***

So there you have it. You may not like these reasons for your lack of success and achievement, and that's okay. What I do know is that those who are on the path of achieving their goals and improving their lives either don't have these issues or they're doing more work to alleviate them than you are. If any or all of the above reasons for failure offend you, that only means they're hitting a nerve and you still don't want to take corrective action.

A Final Word

The solutions to life problems are often simple. Implementing those solutions might be difficult, but what in life worth having has ever come simple or easily? On that note, I'll leave you with another of one my cardinal rules and leave you to figure out the rest for yourself, for after all... *It's your life.* You can have and be anything you want in this life, provided you are willing to put in the work necessary to achieve it. The world only owes you 2 things: a place to live & a place to die. Everything in between is up to you.

The first step to ***getting your mind right*** is to look at where you are now and determine if you're really happy with your circumstances. If you are then God bless you – keep doing what you're doing. But if you take a cold hard look at your life and you admit to yourself that you want to have, do and or become more in your life, then you're going to have to also admit that *more* is exactly what you're going to have to do.

Again let me reiterate that this is not going to be an easy process. As the saying goes, "Success lies on the other side of your comfort zone." No muscle ever got bigger without pain. No success was ever achieved without sacrifice, and to paraphrase Frederick Douglass, without struggle there is no progress.

Define what you want in life. Know that success leaves clues and no other human being is any better than you. You have to have the mindset that if one person succeeds you too can succeed. What makes them any better than you? Okay, someone may have had more breaks than you. Someone may have had more help than you.

But what's stopping you from finding people who can help you? The harder you work towards your goals, the more opportunities, or "breaks" you will find opening themselves up to you. You cannot concern yourself with what someone else has versus what you have except for knowing what you need to get it for yourself. Getting those breaks and opportunities is where *your work* comes in.

Know that you will be tested in order to prove yourself worthy of the things you want to achieve. If you encounter an obstacle and quit then what you wanted was never meant to be yours. On the other hand, if you give something all that you possibly could, then dug deeper past your initial pain and discomfort and moved a little further but still didn't get it, then perhaps that thing still wasn't meant to be yours.

You must know that just because you want something (or someone) that desire alone is not enough. You have to have faith that God, the universe, or whatever you deem your higher power to be has a greater plan for you, and those setbacks may just be the learning experiences you need to discover the path and destiny that's actually meant to be yours. Never forget that difficult does not equal impossible.

When you buckle down and dedicate yourself to bettering yourself by reading, and studying and learning whatever it is you need to better yourself – and go about implementing in your daily life what you are learning, you will find yourself gaining both traction and momentum.

The traction keeps you moving and the momentum will give you increasing speed along the way.

Your attitude is the most important element in getting your mind right. You can't get your mind right if you have a poor attitude. But if you live with an attitude of gratitude, your path won't be as hard as if you had an ungrateful, negative or selfish attitude. Be grateful for waking up. Be grateful for having a job to go to, and if you don't have a job, be grateful for being able to go out and look for one. Be grateful for the people in your life – even those who work against you. Think of them like, well... dumbbells! What is the function of a dumbbell? You are to use its dead weight to work against your muscles in order to strengthen them.

Finally, you must have an attitude of expectancy. Expect to achieve your goals. Expect that good things are supposed to happen to you. Expect that blessings are supposed to rain down upon you! **DO NOT** confuse having an attitude of expectancy with having a sense of entitlement. Having an attitude of expectancy means believing you will have what you want. Having a sense of entitlement means believing what you want should just be given to you, and unfortunately, life doesn't work that way.

I believe in you, but **you must believe in you more.** I'm still in the process of "getting my mind right," and I've got a long way to go to get to where I want to be, but I'm so far better off than where I was when I first embarked upon this journey.

Maybe reading this book is the first step on your journey. If it is, I want you to know that you have a great many wonderful experiences ahead of you and I am honored to be a part of your journey. If this book is just another guide along the way, then you've likely experienced the valleys as well as the peaks and I hope this book has helped you to climb to those peaks a lot faster and stronger and I am honored to be a part of your journey as well.

I wish you success, and never forget... *FORTUNE FAVORS THE BRAVE!*

God Bless.
HRJR